I Don't Follow Signs and Wonders...

They Follow Me!

Charles ♥ Frances Hunter

Published by
HUNTER BOOKS
201 McClellan Road
Kingwood, Texas 77339, U.S.A

BOOKS BY CHARLES ♥ FRANCES HUNTER

A CONFESSION A DAY KEEPS THE DEVIL AWAY
ANGELS ON ASSIGNMENT
ARE YOU TIRED?
BORN AGAIN! WHAT DO YOU MEAN?
COME ALIVE
DON'T LIMIT GOD
FOLLOW ME
GO, MAN, GO
GOD IS FABULOUS
GOD'S ANSWER TO FAT...LOOSE IT!
GOD'S CONDITIONS FOR PROSPERITY
HANDBOOK FOR HEALING
HANG LOOSE WITH JESUS
HIS POWER THROUGH YOU
HOT LINE TO HEAVEN
HOW TO HEAL THE SICK
HOW TO MAKE YOUR MARRIAGE EXCITING
I DON'T FOLLOW SIGNS AND WONDERS...THEY FOLLOW ME!
IF YOU REALLY LOVE ME
IMPOSSIBLE MIRACLES
MEMORIZING MADE EASY
MY LOVE AFFAIR WITH CHARLES
NUGGETS OF TRUTH
POSSESSING THE MIND OF CHRIST
P.T.L.A. (Praise the Lord, Anyway!)
SIMPLE AS A.B.C.
SINCE JESUS PASSED BY
the fabulous SKINNIE MINNIE RECIPE BOOK
SUPERNATURAL HORIZONS (from Glory to Glory)
THE TWO SIDES OF A COIN
THIS WAY UP!
WHY SHOULD "I" SPEAK IN TONGUES???

ISBN 0-917726-92-8

Scripture quotations are taken from:
The New King James Version, used throughout unless otherwise stated.
    *1979, 1980, 1982, 1983 by Thomas Nelson, Inc., Nashville, Tennessee.
The Authorized King James Version (KJV)
The Living Bible, Paraphrased (TLB), *1971 Tyndale House Publishers, Wheaton, Ill.

TABLE OF CONTENTS

For information about Charles and
Frances Hunter's Healing Explosions,
video teaching tapes, audio tapes, and
books, or foreign languages for missions
training, write to:

CHARLES ♥ FRANCES HUNTER
201 McClellan Road
Kingwood, Texas 77339, U.S.A

FOREWORD

"And there are also many things that Jesus did, which if they were written one by one, I suppose that even the world itself could not contain the books that would be written. Amen" (John 21:25).

Recently we began to reread some of the miracles which have been reported in our tabloids (newspapers), and the Holy Spirit spoke and said, "These miracles cannot die with the tabloids, they must be preserved in a book, even though there is not room enough to contain them all." That's when He directed our next book to be chronicled, and the title came, *"I Don't Follow Signs and Wonders...They Follow Me!"*

Not only are we going to share what has happened to and through us, but we are going to share some signs and wonders which have happened through others who have taken our "How To Heal the Sick" training and who are stepping out in faith and becoming a believer of action! Don't stop until you have read the last page because it's a fabulous collection of signs and wonders.

This is the hour of the believer when God is calling every believer to come off of their comfortable soft padded pews, and begin to be men and women who actually cause the words of Jesus to become a reality in today's living!

God has put into our hearts and souls that we must teach the believer that "If Charles and Frances can do it, you can do it, too!" ...and also "If Jesus did it, you can do it, too, only you can do greater things because He said so in His Word!" (John 14:12).

This is the very core of our being. This is the very breath of our lives. Our teachings on HOW TO HEAL THE SICK are the tools which have been used worldwide to encourage the believer that this is HIS hour!

Jesus said, "Go therefore and make disciples of all the nations..." (Matthew 29:18).

During our Healing Explosions we have trained thousands through the books and video tapes HOW TO HEAL THE SICK; that in the name of Jesus and by the power of the Holy Spirit we can accomplish signs, wonders and miracles even in the twentieth century. "Jesus Christ is the same yesterday, today, and forever" (Hebrews 13:8). He has not changed one single bit!

Many of the people who have had their lives changed through these exciting Healing Explosions, have written or told us what happened to them as they took the Bible as a personal challenge from the Lord Jesus. We are intertwining their stories along with ours throughout this book so you will believe beyond a shadow of a doubt that signs and wonders actually do follow ALL believers, and that includes YOU!

As you read through our stories and the testimonies from other people, you will see that "God is no respecter of persons". These testimonies are from young children, teenagers, young adults, middle-aged men and women, people from every denomination and nation and every walk of life. Many of them have heard of the great signs and wonders which have happened at past Healing Explosions from friends and neighbors and loved ones who have been touched by the mighty hand of God!

It would be impossible for us to write about every sign and wonder which has followed us over the years, simply because there wouldn't be enough room to contain them, nor can we remember them all, because they have happened in such astronomical numbers.

It would also be impossible for us to print each and every letter of testimony which has been written about the many great signs and wonders which have occurred since our teachings on HOW TO HEAL THE SICK began circling the globe; but we have selected some of our most favorite signs and wonders stories and a small sampling of what has happened across the world by ordinary everyday miracle-working disciples because they have been trained "how to heal the sick" and have attended one or more of the great Healing Explosions in their areas. Many of them have actually had to travel across the globe to be in attendance, and are now holding Healing Explosions in their own countries, which is exactly as Jesus planned it.

Some of these letters will be printed in their entirety. Some of them will be excerpted. Since they have not been written by professional writers, some of them have not used proper grammar, yet because of the anointing of the Holy Spirit upon them, they need to be read from beginning to end in order to see what has happened and how these signs and wonders are appearing.

May this inspire you to go and do likewise!

Charles and Frances Hunter

Chapter One

SIGNS AND WONDERS FOLLOW
...AND FOLLOW ...AND FOLLOW

by Frances

I LOVE THE SUPERNATURAL! I guess one of the reasons is that I was born into the kingdom of God through a supernatural experience. As a result, I associate all things concerning God and Jesus Christ totally with the supernatural.

How well I remember the night God wiped all the printing off of the page of my Bible where Psalm 23 was written, and revealed a snow white page. Then He proceeded to write on it in the brilliant red blood of Jesus Christ!

The words He wrote were life-changing: "Frances Gardner (that was my name then), I love you!" Five words were all that He wrote, but it was enough to make me realize for the first time in my life that God loved me as an individual, and not just as "the world".

Charles' life was also totally changed through the supernatural. After thirty-one years as a leader of a church, he was completely transformed and baptized with the fire of the Holy Spirit by making a simple statement to God: "Take all of my life and make me spiritually what YOU want me to be!" And he was transformed in the twinkling of an eye after all those years of trying to live a holy life!

It was only natural that our love affair should be supernatural. We met and married without ever having a date, or ever seeing each other from the time we met until we were married just eighty-eight days later. These stories are told in previous books, *God is Fabulous, Follow Me* and *My Love Affair with Charles.*

And I suppose that it was only natural that our walk with God would be totally in the supernatural! God had ordained from the very beginning of time that we should walk in the miraculous!

Many of the supernatural happenings in our lives are recorded in our first thirty-two books, but because God is increasing the tempo of His supernatural acts, and there is a heavenly acceleration going on today which has never been experienced before, we have been encouraging other people to walk in the supernatural of God at all times.

I was rereading our book *Since Jesus Passed By* recently and was amazed to discover something that we wrote in 1973. The Holy Spirit knew then what we would be doing today:

"The desire of our hearts has always been to breathe a real discipleship into the lives of others. It's fun to see congregations get all excited, but before we received the baptism with the Holy Spirit, we sometimes wondered what happened after we left. Did they continue on, or did they drop back into lukewarmness in just a little while? The enduement of power from on high which comes with the baptism with the Holy Spirit calls people out of the ranks to serve God as one of those Paul spoke about 'who will, in turn, pass them (great truths) on to others.'

"In the revivals of the past, people have often worshipped an 'idol', and felt God could move only through an 'idol', but certainly not through an ordinary individual. We probably thought the same thing ourselves years ago, but through the power of the Holy Spirit wherein we KNOW we have the very power of God in our lives, the ordinary layman is reaching out to touch others, and Spirit-filled pastors are discovering the Holy Spirit is bestowing the gifts of the Spirit in generous quantities to those who will ask. An 'idol' is not necessary - only the moving of God's Holy Spirit."

There is a scripture which is so burned in our hearts we can hardly think of anything else. It is as though God placed a red-hot brand on our hearts which contained the Great Commission of the Bible.

"Go into all the world and preach the gospel to every creature. He who believes and is baptized will be saved; but he who does not believe will be condemned. And these signs will follow those who believe: In My name they will cast out demons; they will speak with new tongues; they will take up serpents, and if they drink anything deadly, it will by no means hurt them; they will lay hands on the sick, and they will recover" (Mark 16:15-18).

We live it, we eat it, we sleep it, we love it, we think it, we speak it and we do it at all times!

Although this scripture has been there all the time, it seems as though God has shined down a bright light on it, and the entire world is coming alive to the fact that each of us must be out there doing what Jesus told us to do!

Many times Christians think that going to church is running to the altar every Sunday with the same problems as they had the week before, then going out and living through the week just as they did previously, and then returning to the altar the next Sunday with the same problems! It can be a continuous thing every week of the year until we learn to walk in the way God planned.

Today believers are becoming real "doers" of the Word. And wherever we have taken this message of the believer doing the work, it has spread like wildfire. There is revival going on all over the world.

We're going to ask you to walk with us through a portion of two years of our lives. The same signs and wonders that follow us want to follow YOU! Come along and have fun!

Starting with the month of January, 1986, we want you to run with us through some of our exciting meetings and Healing Explosions. We started off preparing for the Healing Explosion in Jacksonville, and eight days in Florida provided a supernatural harvest of some of the most tremendous miracles we have ever seen.

We attended a pastors' and leaders' meeting at Charlotte, N.C. and met the pastor of the Calvary Assembly of God church in Ormond Beach, Florida. He invited us to come to his church on the one night still available in our Florida schedule and insisted he could put a good meeting together in four days. More than 1,000 people showed up to jam the church which shows that a good meeting can be put together quickly if you really get the vision.

We talked for a few minutes concerning the miraculous things God is doing today. Then we asked if there was anyone in the audience who had tremendous pain. We repeated the statement so everyone would know we only wanted those who had very serious pain in their body at that particular moment.

Over on the right side of the church a girl lifted her hand. She was a Southern Baptist girl who had gone to the doctor that afternoon for her final check-up before surgery on Wednesday. On her way to the doctor she had seen the sign in front of the church which said, "Miracle Service Tonight with Charles and Frances Hunter".

After she passed the sign, the Holy Spirit dropped a thought into her mind. She might not have realized it was the Holy Spirit, but it was. The thought which went through her mind was, "Could God really do it today? Does God still heal today? Would God heal me?" She thought about this and pondered about the teaching she had previously received on whether or not God still heals today. She decided she had nothing to lose, so she had some friends bring her to the church that night.

The ushers assisted her up onto the stage because she was in such agony she could not walk by herself. Pain was obvious with every step she took and every word she spoke. A chiropractor was in the audience and we asked him to examine her. He reconfirmed the fact that she had an area of great spasm there which indicated a ruptured disc. This was on Monday night before the scheduled surgery on Wednesday.

The Bible says we can "call into being those things which do not exist as though they did", so we sat her down in a chair and commanded a new disc to form in her back. Her legs were made uneven by the pull in the back and when the supernatural power of God went into her spine, her leg went back into proper position. Before we ever told her to get up, the girl jumped out of her seat and said, "It doesn't hurt any more! It doesn't hurt any more! It doesn't hurt any more!" She began to run back and forth across the stage. The entire church stood up and screamed with excitement!

The rostrum was raised three steps above the auditorium floor, so we suggested she walk up and down the three stairs to make real sure she was healed. She shocked the entire church, but probably most of all the chiropractor as she very slowly walked to the back of the stage and then ran all the way across the stage and LEAPED out into the audience, landed on her feet and took off running.

The chiropractor put his hand over his eyes and cried, "Oh, no!" She kept right on running with absolutely no pain, and the chiropractor said, "If God hadn't healed her, she would have just exploded her back!" Praise God, it didn't explode her back, but it did "explode" the church. Faith rose up so high that scores of miracles followed this first one!

She came forward and received the baptism with the Holy Spirit at the end of the service and did not need the surgery.

Right after that there was a man who was eighty-two years old who was all shriveled up with arthritis and didn't look like he weighed much more than eighty-two pounds. He had had his stomach removed, he had atrophied muscles in his legs, arms and feet, and was full of pain and arthritis. He had not been able to eat for a long, long time.

We ministered healing to the arthritis first by casting out the spirit, and then we commanded a new stomach to form in his body and all pain to leave. This old man got up and danced on the stage because all the pain was gone! He was so excited! He said he was going to go right home and eat black-eyed peas, cornbread and buttermilk. Hallelujah! (Note: We were back in the area a month later, and his friends reported that was exactly what he did - gorged himself on black-eyed peas, cornbread and buttermilk!)

It was a night of great rejoicing as many were healed of all kinds of diseases, including one man who was dying with cancer. He could hardly walk. He was in tremendous pain and had a horrible death-like color. We commanded the foul spirit of cancer to come out in the name of Jesus, commanded all the cancer cells to die, and commanded the marrow of his bones to begin to manufacture good red blood.

He walked away with his cane in the air, color had returned to his face, and he was rejoicing because he had absolutely no pain left! God continues to do the miraculous and signs and wonders will follow the believer, if we'll just get out there and fulfill the Great Commission.

Then the book of Acts moved to St. Augustine, Florida where the so-called "fountain of youth" is located, and we told them we had found the fountain of youth in Jesus Christ. A medical doctor and two chiropractors were there so we had three doctors examining those to whom we were ministering.

One of the most exciting miracles concerned a beautiful black lady who had been in an automobile accident thirteen months prior. She was in excruciating pain in both her neck and back. We asked one of the chiropractors to examine her and he said, "I don't have to. She's my patient and after treating her for thirteen months, I told her that there is nothing else I can do for her."

He had done everything he knew how to do, and she was still in agony. We simply commanded total healing in the name of Jesus, and what power there is in that name! All pain left instantly! She stood on the stage bending in all directions and doing all sorts of contortions and was completely convinced that she was totally healed. She walked off the stage, and when she got to the aisle leading up the side of the church to her seat, she had a "Pentecostal fit" that would have thrilled anyone because her back and neck were going in all directions at the same time. She had absolutely no pain whatsoever. She had walked off of the stage in such a dignified manner that the "Pentecostal fit" was a shock to everyone, but what a message it carried!

Another one we called up was a lady who was wearing a neck brace. She was pale, full of pain and had been bedridden for three years. After she was examined by all three doctors, they agreed there were three ruptured discs there. She had absolutely no range of motion whatsoever. We commanded three new discs to come into place, and she began to laugh and move her head and then laugh and move her head more and more and she continued to laugh all throughout the service. Some people really get Holy Ghost joy when they are healed and it shows all over them and melts the hearts of the audience as well. She was still laughing when she left the church.

Dr. Jim Hayes, a general practitioner in the St. Augustine area, was the medical doctor who had been assisting us on the stage. After he watched so many people being healed, he asked if he could possibly be healed. And, of course, you KNOW what we said!

He told us he had fallen from a second story building at the age of four. The fall had impacted his spine and as a result he had lower back spasms and chronic pain. He then said that for the past year he had been unable to lift anything, walk quickly or even bend over without experiencing severe spasm and pain. He had been under the care of an orthopedic surgeon and an osteopath for about six months with some improvement, but was still quite limited by pain and stiffness.

He said in a letter which he mailed to us shortly after that, "When you laid hands on me and grew out my right leg and commanded my pelvis to rotate and my back to be normal in the name of Jesus, I was instantly healed!

"As you remember, I immediately bent over and touched my toes with my knees unbent - something I never was able to do. I have been sharing this miracle with my patients and friends ever since and I have been able to do all the things I couldn't do for years without pain. Praise God!

"I became a Christian during my first year of college about sixteen years ago at the age of seventeen. After graduating from medical school, I received the baptism with the Holy Spirit eight years ago and came to the realization that miracles and healing had not passed away as I had been taught.

"When we were first married in 1977, Barbara and I dedicated our future children to the Lord. We believed He would give us children in His perfect time. After five years of seeking Him and trusting Him but still not having any children, we sought medical help. We underwent many tests and procedures and were finally told our situation was hopeless. Every time I sought Him, He would tell me we *would* have children but would never say when.

"The healing of my back was so inspiring to us that we watched your video course, HOW TO HEAL THE SICK. We heard you share that there were many 'Hunter babies' in the world and I realized God was leading us to have you pray for us in Jacksonville.

"As you recall, on Valentine's Day after the doctors' panel in Jacksonville, Barbara and I asked for prayer to be healed of infertility after eight years of marriage. The Lord spoke through you, Frances, and said Barbara would conceive and deliver within one year. We both fell out under the power simultaneously. I knew God had finally answered our prayers. Barbara became pregnant within a month! Hallelujah!

"Since the Healing Explosion in Jacksonville, my ministry has literally exploded and I have been leading many patients to accept Jesus as their personal Lord and Savior. Some have been healed and baptized in the Holy Spirit as well.

"Jesus surely is the GREAT PHYSICIAN.

Love, Jim and Barbara"

I will never forget the day Dr. Hayes called to let me know Barbara was pregnant. He didn't even have to use the telephone - I could have heard him all the way from Florida to Texas. And again when their little boy Joshua was born just nine months later, his joy could not be contained! Nothing is ever dull when you're walking in the supernatural with God!

Shortly after this we were in Media, Pennsylvania. One of the gifts of the Spirit is the word of knowledge, and when exercised it can really bring dramatic results. I had a word of knowledge about someone who had excruciating pain in the lower part of their lumbar spine. It was a very sharp, clear and distinct word of knowledge, so clear that I repeated it four or five times. Over and over again I said, "Someone here has a horrible pain in the lower part of their lumbar spine. Don't sit there, come up here because God wants to heal you right now.

Even though I said this many times, no one responded to the call. Finally I said, "It doesn't make any difference whether you answer or not, God is speaking."

At the end of the service a policeman from the city of Philadelphia came up and said, "Did I blow it?"

I said, "What do you mean?"

He replied, "I was the one with that awful back

problem. Every time you mentioned it I was covered with goose pimples, but I kept thinking, 'She's not talking to me, she's not talking to me'. Is it too late for me to get my healing?"

Of course I said, "No, your healing was just delayed awhile!" He told us he had been injured ten years before and had not been able to work. We ministered to him and he was totally and completely healed when we grew his leg out. It wasn't the leg that grew out, he had a pinched nerve in his back which made his leg look short, but when the back was healed the leg came back to the normal position. He bent every which way trying to make his back hurt but - there was no pain! What joy! What rejoicing!

Whenever you are in an audience and a word of knowledge is called out for YOU, be sure to respond. When an audience sees that God has personally picked you for a miraculous healing, their response is incredible and their faith will rise to new heights for their own healing.

Our mail is always exciting for us to open when we come home from a trip, because we never know what exciting news it is going to bring. The following letter thrilled our hearts because it confirms what God's Word has to say about giving and proves that all miracles are not healings, but lots of other areas as well:

"At your Healing Explosion in Denver we wrote a check for $100. We had $130.00 left in our checking account. My husband is a realtor so we live on commission. He had nothing under contract with no income expected. I practically had a nervous breakdown with creditors calling and Christmas coming. I vacillated between trusting God as our provider and yelling at my husband to do *something*.

"Well, God was and is faithful. On December 8, we received an unexpected gift of $1,000.00. Praise God!"

I sincerely hope this story edifies you and others. God even takes care of weak doubters if they practice faithfulness to His spiritual laws.

Another letter brought an exciting little tid-bit. "A fallen away Christian (he had studied for the priesthood) collapsed at work because of internal bleeding. At the hospital they filled him full of barium, x-rayed him and said he had a tumor in his stomach. I prayed for him the way you teach and about a week later, when he was checked at a different hospital, there was no tumor. It really 'rattled his cage' and did wonders for my self-confidence!"

Let's go to Chattanooga!

Joppa Wiese is a miracle! He came to a meeting dying from heart failure. The pastor of the church whispered to us at the beginning of the service that he was a very sick man, so we called him up quickly, laid hands on him, and he fell out under the power.

The worship and praise continued, but my spirit was not satisfied because I felt the miracle had not yet been completed, so at the conclusion of the praise and worship we called him forward again.

At that time he told us he also suffered from severe diabetes and emphysema. That triggered in my spirit a story of a most unusual healing that had occurred several years ago at our meeting in a very small town in Pennsylvania.

We were in a Mennonite church and I had a tremendous word of knowledge about a very severe heart problem being healed! God spoke very clearly and said He was giving someone a new heart, so I asked if there was anyone there who had an extremely serious heart problem. It was difficult to understand the response because where I had anticipated one person with this problem, more than twenty people came forward. This never bothers me because I know in my spirit that God has a whole warehouse of spare parts. General Motors, as well as all other manufacturers, make spare parts for their products, and God is much smarter than all of the business geniuses in the world so I know that He can give you a brand new part. As a matter of fact, Charles often says I have more new parts than originals.

We went down the line laying hands on everyone and speaking a creative miracle of a new heart into each of them. Everyone in the line fell under the power of God except one man. He looked quizzically around at me as if to say, "Why didn't I fall down?" and I said, "Don't worry, that's all right, you got a new heart!"

They all went back to their seats, and we continued the service when I noticed a lot of activity around this man who had not gone under the power. We tried to have it not interrupt the service, but suddenly we saw someone run out of the church and return with an oxygen tank. About this time I decided I'd better get down there, so I walked up to him and said, "Brother, I didn't lay hands on you for a heart attack, I laid hands on you for a new heart!"

He immediately fell forward and said, "Nitroglycerine, nitroglycerine!" They placed a nitroglycerine tablet under his tongue and his son said, "He has emphysema and diabetes as well!"

I laid hands on him and commanded a new pancreas and new lungs! By this time Charles came down off of the stage. After looking at him, we decided we should get an ambulance, so the church secretary ran to call one.

We asked the entire audience to get on their knees and pray, because we knew a man's life was at stake. All of them immediately began to fervently pray. One of the things we did not know was that this town was so small it did not have a hospital, or a doctor, or a paramedic, so they had to call a volunteer group about thirty miles away.

We prayed and prayed and sometimes I wonder if I was praying like the rest of them because I was asking God to get that ambulance there in a hurry and get him out of the church. I certainly didn't want him dying in a miracle service!

Finally the paramedics arrived after what seemed an interminable length of time! I felt we could breathe a little easier because when they rushed in, it was like a "D-Day" invasion! Seven of them ran to the man, began giving him oxygen and doing various other things. Suddenly everyone in the church heard them say on their portable telephone, "Patient unstable! We do not know when we can move him!"

Do you have any idea how the heart of an evangelist beats when you have a critical situation like that on your hands? I thought, "Oh, no!" Then the entire congregation doubled up on their prayers, because there is no way you can continue a service when there is a situation like that present.

Read what Charles saw during these tense moments:

"I have seen the spirits of two different people when they left their bodies in death. I was watching the paramedics frantically working on the man and at a point when it seemed they were especially alarmed, I saw the man's spirit leave his body like a vapor. It went up until it was half in the body and half above the body, moving upward.

"I said, 'Spirit of life, go back into him in the Name of Jesus!' His spirit went back, but no sooner had it re-entered than up it came again, this time going completely above the body. I felt like trying to push it back in with my hands, but I knew the only power which could do this, so again I said, 'In the Name of Jesus, spirit of life, go back into him!'

"Again it went back into the body. This was repeated seven times, and the seventh time it stayed in the body and this was apparently the time the paramedics found him stabilized enough to take him to the ambulance and on to the hospital."

"These twelve Jesus sent out and commanded them, saying:... Heal the sick, cleanse the lepers, RAISE THE DEAD, cast out demons. Freely you have received, freely give" (Matthew 10:5,8).

We breathed a sigh of relief.

Then what do you do after that? It was now quite late, and yet we knew there were many people who had come for a healing, so we said, "If any of you would like for us to lay hands on you, we'll be glad to right now if you'll come forward."

We had the shortest healing line we've ever had in the history of our ministry! We never saw so many people go out the door as fast as they did! I'm not sure I blame them. We laid hands on the few who were left (and it was a huge church), and then went to bed.

The town is so small there is no motel or hotel, so we stayed in a room in the church. About midnight there was a knock on our door. It was the pastor and the son of the man who had the heart attack. The young man said, "My father told me not to go home tonight until I had personally delivered a message to you. He said for me to tell you that he still has faith to believe he received a new heart!"

I screamed even at that late hour, "He got it, he got it!" After going through what he had just experienced, if he still had faith to believe he had a new heart, then I knew that the devil had not been able to rob him of what God had given him. The pastor continued and told me that the man had been in a Baltimore hospital waiting for a quadruple bypass for several months. Finally an opening had come, but because they did not feel he could live through it, the doctors told him to come home and make arrangements for his funeral. The pastor heard the news and went over and invited him to the miracle service, telling him he believed he could be healed! He had a massive heart attack instead.

My spirit leaped within me even at this news, because I knew that the man had not lost his faith. It is at times like this that the devil loves to come in and rob us of anything and everything God wants us to have, but that man absolutely did not listen to anything the devil had to say.

The local doctors called for a heart specialist because they knew he could not be moved to Baltimore. They took x-rays the next morning. Then they took another series of x-rays because they could not believe what they saw! Instead of the old worn-out heart that needed a quadruple bypass, they said he had the heart of a "twenty-five-year-old athlete!"

They kept him in the hospital for additional tests and after five days they could find no trace of diabetes in his body even though he had been using insulin for thirty-seven years! They checked his lungs for emphysema and found not a trace left! Glory to God, NOTHING IS IMPOSSIBLE WITH GOD, if we can just believe! The following Sunday he was back at the same church dancing in the Spirit with the pastor on the stage and sharing his testimony of what the Lord had done for him.

We shared this exciting miracle at a meeting in Florida the next fall and a woman from this man's church was there and reported they had just had their church's annual picnic, and this man was the star player on the softball team!

When I called Joppa Wiese up the second time, he stood there while I related this entire story. Then he told me two additional facts. He also had diabetes and emphysema! God had a special purpose in reminding me of the story so it could build Joppa's faith! His blood pressure was 250/114 when he was last seen by the doctor who had told his wife that Joppa's heart had enlarged to eighteen centimeters across and was leaking blood. His doctor had told him it was too late for a transplant.

He experienced a miracle of God at that meeting. When he fell under the power of God the second time he said suddenly he could breathe deeply and had no pain in his chest whatsoever. He went to the doctor's office the next day and when his doctor saw him he turned white, almost fainted and said, "What happened to you?"

Joppa simply replied, "God healed me!" Tests revealed his blood pressure was 127/82, the doctor heard a strong heart-beat and the x-rays showed the heart had come down in size and the lungs had cleared. Joppa is again working as a jeweler, although his desire leans more and more every day towards being an evangelist.

A letter from his doctor is in our files. He said, "I am writing you at the request of one of my patients, Joppa Wiese, who in my opinion experienced a 'miracle' in that he was literally at death's door and following this event at church, the state of his health was improved to an extent that was unexplainable by the laws of modern medicine.

"When he was initially seen by me, his congestive heart failure was as severe as any patient I have seen in twenty years and nothing short of a heart transplant would have kept him alive. I explained this moribund state to Mr. Wiese and his wife and offered to refer him to one of the University Medical Centers but Joppa declined and told me at that time that he would leave his living or dying up to the Lord.

"My response was that the Lord must have had reasons unknown to us all for keeping him alive and that I would do all that I knew to do and leave it up to the Lord as to whether he lived or died.

"Mr. Wiese will return to work next week and without a doubt could never have survived his heart failure without the Lord's intervention. It was indeed an act of God."

One sign and wonder follows another. That is why we do what the Bible tells us, "Tell often what the Lord has done for you!" In sharing the miracle of one man, another man got healed of exactly the same problems. And the fact that they happen to us is good enough reason for you to believe they can follow after you as well!

Sometimes signs and wonders will follow you even if you are not there. The letters we receive would lift the spirits of anyone, because often these letters may be just the divine medicine you need to heal whatever your problems are, whether they are spiritual, mental, or physical. Maybe you don't have all the problems involved in some of these letters, but there may be a little something in them which will trigger everything you need in your life. God has a unique way of making one person's testimony change another person's life!

Sometimes a person's life begins at forty, according to the old adage, but in my case it began at forty-nine when I met Jesus, and this particular Canadian discovered her life began at age thirty, when she saw it fall apart.

"I just decided to take this opportunity to write you a note to tell you of the miraculous changes that have taken place in my life in just two short months!!

"I'll start with my thirtieth birthday two months ago. Most people dread their thirtieth birthday, but not me! I was convinced that I was not getting older, I was getting better! That's when the bombshell hit - the company I work for announced they were closing down the plant where I work (at a job I really, really enjoy) and my husband whom I adore left me!! He said he couldn't handle my attitude towards 'life, the universe and everything'! All on my birthday! Great, eh? (Oops - I should say 'huh?' since you're American). Needless to say, I really thought I was cracking up! I tried to get an appointment with a psychiatrist, but here in Hamilton there is a six month waiting list unless you have slashed your wrists already. My family doctor put me on Valium (which I didn't want to take, having had lots of drug problems before). I took it though.

"One day, on my way home from work, I happened to get on the bus with Michael (an acquaintance who was 'one of those born-again weirdos'). He saw that I was hysterical and asked me what was wrong. I told him the whole sad story, including what my husband said about my 'attitude' problem.

"All Mike said was, 'I know something that will really help your attitude'. I knew he was talking about church - something I'd avoided like the plague for thirty years!!!

"I said, 'Let me think about it.' But God was already working on me. Two weeks later I attended their Tuesday night Bible study class.

"When I got there, people were going, 'Praise the Lord' and 'Thank You, Jesus' right out loud! And if this wasn't weird enough, the pastor announced that this was the first night of a seven week course on 'How to Heal the Sick' by Charles and Frances Hunter.

"Healing the sick? Who were these people kidding! But I was brought up to be polite, and so I couldn't leave until the evening was over.

"Well, I still thought it was all pretty weird, but Frances, you were a hoot! (That's 'funny' in Canadian). And to top it all off, you really seemed to believe that the sick could be healed. I was fascinated by your sincerity and I came again the next week.

"Charles, your explanation about turning on a light switch made real sense to me! I went to the Sunday services and enjoyed it, but when Michael turned to me and said, 'Beth, don't you think it's time that you accept Christ as your Savior?' my first impulse was to run away! I wanted to yell 'NO!' - but I couldn't. Because if my life was ever going to change for the better, there was only one way to do it, and I knew that. I felt a deep sense of peace wash over me as I repeated the 'sinner's prayer' with Mike. I praise the Lord many times daily for making me realize that I needed Him in my life if it was ever to be worthwhile!

"I continued going to the video classes, and learning from both of you. Thank you!

"During the session about growing out arms and

legs, the pastor suggested we should try it during our coffee break. We paired off and tried it. Sure enough, one of my legs was about a half inch shorter than the other one. We commanded it to grow out and it did! But the really miraculous healing was in one woman who came every week, walking with two canes. She was healed completely - no longer needs the canes - and looks ten years younger now that the pain is gone! Praise the Lord!!!

"At this point, I have to explain something. I was born with something like club feet. I couldn't walk properly until I was about nine years old and they operated on both my legs. After that I could walk all right, but my feet turned out. Duck Feet! I could only straighten them with a great deal of pain. Well, that evening, after growing out of legs, I was on my way home from church and it felt like the heel was coming off my shoe or something. I checked it, and my shoes were both fine. But something looked strange. I couldn't figure out what it was - and then it hit me (like a ton of bricks!) MY FEET WERE STRAIGHT!!! The Lord not only grew out my leg, but straightened everything in both my feet as well! Oh, what a beautiful Lord He is!

"I showed my husband (we were seeing each other about once a week) that my feet were straight - but he didn't really understand, and still avoids talking about Jesus or even church - but we all know the power of prayer! Praise God!

"He is moving back home next week, and I just know, deep down inside, that everything is going to be just fine. He loves the change in my attitude, and eventually he will want what I have, Jesus as his Savior, too!

"Charles, Frances, I can't say that all of this wouldn't have happened without you, because I'm sure the Lord had been working in me for a very long time.

But I can say that it would never have happened NOW, if I hadn't met the two of you through your video series (and if I hadn't met a bus driver named Mike that day), because you fascinated me enough to make me keep coming back! Thank you both!"

Signs and wonders follow even through video!

God takes us into interesting and unusual places to do interesting and unusual miracles. Such was a time when we ministered in a large Dallas, Texas camp meeting in a tent on a very hot July 5th. There are times when God "shows off" on television, and this was a most unique and powerful demonstration of His Spirit and power.

We called for people who had severe pain in their body. One of the first was a lady who had a rib so separated from the rest you could put three fingers between two of the ribs. Dr. Roy LeRoy, a well-known chiropractor, was working with us that night. He examined the ribs and confirmed the extent of the separation, and agreed she was in pain.

We grew out her arms and commanded the ribs to go back into place, the muscles, tendons, ligaments, and nerves to be healed, and when she tested by moving her body, there was absolutely no pain. Dr. LeRoy checked her ribs again and said they were perfectly in place!

Wayne Powell was the last one in line after everyone who came forward was healed. The story he told was amazing. He was in a bunker in Vietnam when an 88mm mortar shell made a direct hit on the bunker. He was very seriously wounded, and after extensive surgery and a long time in the military hospital, they could not remove all the shrapnel from his body without causing further complications.

In time the shrapnel in his right leg deteriorated his hip joint, so a plastic hip joint was implanted to help remedy the problem.

As is usually the case, he could not bear his full weight on that joint. Not only that, three discs in his spine were rubbing "bone on bone" so he could not stand straight. He also said they wired him together near the broken hip joint.

He later suffered further injuries in a truck accident in 1985 when he was trapped in a wrecked 3/4 ton pickup truck for an hour. He was hospitalized for a month while he recovered from having his left side crushed. His left shoulder blade was broken like a dish and separated to where you could feel the sunken hole. Dr. LeRoy put his finger in the hole and said there was no shoulder blade where his finger was placed. Wayne also said he didn't have a shoulder blade in the broken place.

Just as we train all our healing teams to say, when he finished telling us all the problems, we said, "That's easy!"

What a dramatic experience we had as the power of God went through him when we grew out his leg and commanded the hip joint to be restored and that part of his body to be healed, IN JESUS' NAME! Then we laid hands on the broken shoulder blade and commanded the bones to come together.

Since he previously had not been able to raise his arm more than half way up, we said, "Lift up your arm," and to his and our delight, the arm dramatically shot straight up. The audience went wild with excitement! That was the first time it had worked since the accident. Then he moved his arm until he could touch the middle of his back. He said his wife had to wash his back because his arm wouldn't reach there.

Then we said, "Test the rest of your body and see what God has done."

He replied, "Where's my chair?" He sat down in it and began to cross his right leg over his left, time and time again, and laughingly he said, "There's not an artificial hip joint made in America that can do that! I haven't been able to do that since 1968!"

It's funny how little things are so important when you can't do them!

Then we said, "Let's see you run down this ramp and into the audience." He looked at us rather peculiarly, then took off running, laughing as he went. We ran down the ramp to meet him and he said he never could do that before. Then we said, "Let's see you run back up the ramp."

He said, "My wife can tell you that I can't even walk up a ramp like that." She came forward saying that she was healed two nights before of arthritis and that he really couldn't walk uphill.

We said, "Let's see which of you can outrun the other!" They dashed off together but he was at the top when she was only half way.

The stage was about eighteen inches higher than the ramp and he put his left leg up on the stage and lifted his entire 185 pounds of weight. He stepped off the stage and did this over and over again. He could hardly believe his hip was working so perfectly.

There was no pain left, his legs and arms were working perfectly and the hip joint seemed like a new one.

We called him a few days later, asking him how he was doing. He said that before his healing when he went up the stairs in his home he had to pull himself up with his arms and almost drag the leg. But NOW he could run up the stairs two steps at a time and still there was no pain; his arm was perfect.

We asked him to have his doctor x-ray his body, examine it, and give us a medical report, at our expense.

Shortly after that, we were with Dr. LeRoy and a medical doctor. When they carefully examined the x-rays, they said, "Look at that shoulder blade! There's not even a hairline break there. Look at that hip socket!" They said the artificial joint was still there, but God had put human cartilage over the joint; a most unusual miracle.

God can do His miracles any way He wants, and that is fine with Wayne Powell because he has had absolutely no problems walking, leaping, and praising God since he received his miracle! Hallelujah!

His daughter Camille testifies: "My Dad always stood crooked before his healing. Now he stands straight!"

Let's hop a plane and go from Dallas to Chicago for a one-night stand, but what a night to remember!

Pastor Bill Blonn of the King's Community Church in South Holland, Illinois, really caught the vision of what Healing Explosions are all about, but more important, what video healing schools can do to a church. He had several healing schools going at the same time, and as a result, he had over 250 people qualified to minister healing. One hundred and twenty of them had just completed the entire series, so we gave out one hundred and twenty healing team certificates. They could hardly wait to minister.

As we started the service, it was obvious that the people who had been trained to heal the sick sent out so much faith that it would have been almost impossible to have walked out of there without being healed.

A couple had come a long way to attend the service. They had never been at a charismatic service and stood there wondering what it was all about when the praise and worship virtually raised the roof of the church. The singing and the participation from the congregation brought a tremendous presence of God during that wonderful part of the service.

Then came the offering time, and they admitted they had never seen people so joyous about giving, but God had ordained all of this to prepare them for the most unexpected of all - their healings!

The husband had broken his back and was sitting in a wheelchair. I stepped down to him, laid my hands on his back and commanded a new spine to come into being. Then I said something as I stood in front of his chair to let him see that God had answered his prayer. I said, "Kick me!" And to everyone's amazement, including both his and mine, he immediately kicked out his leg! I said, "If you can kick that leg, then you can stand up, so in the name of Jesus, stand up."

He stood up!

Then I said, "If you can stand up, then you can walk, so in the name of Jesus, walk!" The place was so jammed it was almost impossible to go anyplace, but because he had discovered he was healed, he began to walk and actually make a path for himself! The audience roared with excitement, and his wife turned up her oxygen because she was so excited she was using up her remaining supply. She had emphysema and had already used up one and one-half tanks of oxygen, and she knew she had to have that last half tank in order to get her home, but God had other plans.

It was easy to discern they were not saved, so they both got saved immediately, because it is hard to turn down Jesus after you've had a miracle. Then we laid hands on her for total healing, and she fell under the power of God, got holy laughter and was totally and completely healed of emphysema and never went back on the oxygen again.

To someone who has been a Pentecostal for years, the above might not seem so supernatural, but when someone who has never seen the supernatural ends up with holy laughter, it is a night never to be forgotten!

They left the service with the wife riding and the husband pushing the wheelchair!

When we began to minister the baptism with the Holy Spirit at the end of the service, a lady stood up to receive. We noticed she was on crutches so we asked the audience if they would mind waiting a minute so she could get healed and not have to walk with crutches.

She had been in an automobile accident and had a broken pelvis and two broken ribs. As we did "the pelvic thing" and commanded the bones to come back in place, she was totally healed. She ran up and down the stairs, the crutches went up in the air and it was a real night of glory.

We are thrilled to have discovered that the churches who show the video healing tapes before we get there have an air of expectancy that is so high anything can happen, and it usually does!

We have also discovered that when you come expecting miracles, you get exactly what you come for. When you expect nothing, you get nothing!

As for me and my house, we agree that we expect signs and wonders to follow!

Chapter Two

THE PLUSES OF JET-LAG

by Frances

Several years ago when we made a few trips overseas, I would come home each time so exhausted and suffering from jet-lag so badly that I made a statement to several friends, "I'll never go overseas again unless God writes me a special delivery letter and hands it to me in person!" Be careful what you say, because God hears your every word!

I really thought we were safe from traveling overseas because of the tremendous physical strain placed upon my body. Then I got healed of diabetes and God delivered a special delivery letter in person! He didn't write it on paper with a pen or pencil, but He wrote it on my heart when He told us to lip-sync the healing video tapes into Spanish as our first foreign language and then go to the country where we would send them.

Jeremiah 33:3 is a scripture many people quote as being something that is always in the far distant future, but it's an alive scripture today. "Call to Me, and I will answer you, and show you great and mighty things, which you do not know!" We believe God is calling upon all of us to let Him show great and mighty things which He wants to do through each of us. We believe we are living in the very last days and that is why the call of God is so strong to show us these great and mighty things!

God spoke to us saying, "Thus far in 1986 I have laid the foundation. During the next two months I will set the dynamite in place. During the first four months of 1987 I will set off an explosion around the world, and then..."

The first stick of spiritual healing dynamite was set in place on December 14, 1986 at the *Coliseo de Salitre* in Bogota, Colombia. God's plans to spread the Miracle Evangelism message to all of South America was very apparent as church leaders from Colombia, Peru, Bolivia, Ecuador and Brazil all converged for the first Healing Explosion in a Spanish-speaking nation.

From the moment the plane landed, we felt electricity in the air. We could feel and sense in our spirits that God was going to do something special. Our plane was two hours late because of authorities questioning some of the passengers aboard as to the reason for their visit to Bogota - was it legitimate, or was it cocaine? This only heightened our excitement about what God was going to do in Bogota!

What a blessing we received at the airport even though we were so late! Over 100 Colombian *Cristianos* were waiting to greet *los Americanos,* and greet us they did! They were singing "I Love You with the Love of the Lord" and "Alleluia" as well as other familiar sounding songs in Spanish; and their love and anticipation was expressed in their tears, hugs and kisses as we made our way through the crowd to get from the plane to cars to the hotel. Never have we been any place where we felt such immediate and tremendous love as we did there!

As we drove to the hotel, we were excited to hear what had been going on before our arrival in Bogota! Over 4,000 had taken the video training on *"How to Heal the Sick",* but because of space limitations, only 1,600 were going to be able to attend the "live" training meetings scheduled before the Explosion.

The pastor shared how one group in his church, before they completed their training with the video, went out on the streets one night and began asking if anyone needed healing. A crowd began to gather and before they finished, over 200 had been healed and 50 were saved as a result of the street healings. Miracle Evangelism works!

So many churches were involved that only a limited number of healing team members were allowed from each congregation. Those with "special credentials" (proper identification indicating they had already watched ALL fourteen and a half hours of video teachings) faithfully attended every training session, grabbing a quick bite to eat and a room temperature bottle of soda pop from food stands on the street. Because of the magnitude of the meetings, the Coffee Commissioner of Colombia sent out trucks to dispense free coffee. Wherever you looked during the breaks between sessions, you could see people praying for each other.

Their excitement to learn more and to be trained in healing was a delight to those of us who attempted to communicate in our inadequate Spanish and through interpreters. Every session was completely packed out wall-to-wall!

The worship and praise was typical of the love of God which permeated the hearts of the Colombian Christians. They put themselves wholeheartedly into praise and worship and we were all lifted up into the very throne room of God at each service.

Basically unadvertised until the last few days, the 9 a.m. "Explosion" on Saturday, December 14 was attended by over 7,000 wild, turned-on Colombians. Not wanting to miss a thing, hundreds stayed throughout the day until the last service ended at 9 o'clock that evening.

The music could be heard and felt a block away as God truly drew more and more into the *Coliseo de Salitre* to experience God's power. The young people of Pastor Cesar Castellano's church both sang and danced in a beautiful panorama throughout both times of worship. Their voices, clapping and cheering were contagious and all were quickly swept up into their enthusiasm.

When we drove up to the coliseum for the first meetings, angels filled the auditorium so full that Charles sensed a bulging of the walls with the power of God. God always sends a great host of angels to every Healing Explosion, and this one seemed to outdo all others in numbers.

As we drove to the coliseum for the second Healing Explosion in one day, we saw people pushing wheelchairs for miles to get to the service. As we walked in, we were greeted with diseases that we had never encountered before, but there was also an expectancy in the entire audience that we had never felt before in any meeting.

Every seat in the great coliseum was filled and every aisle was packed solid with people. It looked like one giant sea of faces squeezed like sardines, but full of faith and belief! The faith of some oozed over onto others! Many people were waiting outside, hoping to get in. It made our hearts cry out because of the needs that were there and the hopeless cripples we saw.

The praise and worship was already in progress and there was such a sense of everyone entering into complete and total adoration of God and Jesus that you could feel the supernatural even while walking to the stage. The people were so excited about what God was going to do that they wanted just to touch us before we walked onto the stage. Believing that they would be healed, they reached out AND THEY WERE HEALED - the Healing Explosion was their point of contact.

As we reached the stage, the pastor asked if we would mind laying hands on those in wheelchairs during the praise and worship. Our spirits leaped within us because we had been wanting to do this during our United States Healing Explosions, and here was our opportunity.

We prayed over the microphone, telling them what we were going to do. We said, "When we touch each of you who are in wheelchairs or crippled, God's healing power will go into you, so get up and walk, in Jesus' name!"

As we stepped off the stage, we both prayed fervently, because the enormity of the moment became a reality to both of us at the same time. We said quickly, "God, if you're not in this, it will be a mess!"

We walked over to the first person in a wheelchair and in very limited Spanish, I said, *"Recibe su sanidad en el nombre de Jesus!"* (Receive your healing in the name of Jesus!) Then I said, *"Levantase!"* (which means "get up").

Neither of us could remember how to say the word "walk". I had studied Spanish fifty-five years previously in high school, but had never used the language. The Holy Spirit really brought it back to my remembrance, but the word "walk" just would not come into my recall pattern. I whispered to Charles who studied Spanish for two years in school, "How do you say 'walk'?"

The Holy Spirit reminded us in a most unusual way. I doubt if there is anyone reading this book who has not heard the little song which goes like this, "La cucaracha, La cucaracha, Ya no puede caminar. Porque no tiene, porque le falta, marijuana que fumar!" Interpreted, that means, "The cockroach, the cockroach. Now he is unable to *walk*. (There was the word we needed!) Because he does not have, because he lacks, marijuana to smoke!" What a silly thing to come back into your mind at a time like this, but it worked!

Charles leaned over and looked at the man and said, "Camina en el nombre de Jesus!" This horribly crippled man immediately walked right out of his wheelchair as if he had never had anything wrong with him. The crowd went wild and faith soared! My mind said, "He must not have been crippled like we thought!" Such faith!

We went to the second person and said exactly the same words. That person walked right out of his wheelchair just as if nothing had been wrong with him. Faith ignited in every person down the line!

We went to number three! Same results! Number 4, number 5, number 6 and right down the line until finally one person failed to rise from their wheelchair. We could hardly believe the gift of faith that had so risen up in us. We thought, "What's wrong with you that you didn't get up?" But we went right on to the next person and the flow kept going as one after another got up and walked. At that point we both felt we could have done anything that Jesus had done including walking on water. Our faith was high!

A little girl with a broken back was brought to the meeting on a stretcher. After we had said the same words to her, she came off of that stretcher and the next thing we knew she was on the stage testifying to what God had done for her. Her little testimony brought tears to the eyes of everyone as she walked even in the cast that immobilized most of her body.

Then there was the blind crippled man who had been brought on a stretcher. As I stretched out my hand toward his eyes, my fingers were about three inches away when he screamed, "I can see! I can see!" In a matter of seconds he was on the stage glorifying God for His miracle power! It was a moment none of us will ever forget!

We didn't stop - we went right down the line, and as soon as they came out of the wheelchairs or dropped their crutches, we turned them over to the healing teams to help them exercise their new walking abilities! More than 100 came out of wheelchairs, stretchers, and braces in one service!

Normally, when someone is healed dramatically or comes out of a wheelchair during a healing service, time is taken to tell the audience about the healing. However, the power of God was so on those who had come that we felt we could not waste even one moment but had to continue as fast as we could through the crowd while the power was so supernatural!

When we had laid hands on the last one, the reality of the magnitude of what God had done fell upon both of us and we cried like babies as we ran back to the stage. Everyone on stage was weeping. As I reached for my purse to get a tissue, my daughter Joan said, "Don't bother, Mother, I've already used them all up!"

Manoel Ferreira, Assistant Superintendent of the General Council of the thirteen million Assemblies of God church members in Brazil wept openly as he said, "Never in all my years of Pentecost have I ever seen anything like this!" And neither had we!

Shortly after this, some 4,000 poured out of the crowd of about 11,000 to receive salvation and the baptism with the Holy Spirit. They ALL began to speak in tongues as the Spirit gave them utterance.

There was no way we could get the people back into the stands after the baptism, so we released the healing

teams to go to the people on the floor and then throughout the audience that remained in the stands. Healings
took place all over that crowded building.

It was time to leave and people were so caught up in
what God was doing they took pieces of clothing off and
threw them at us to touch and return to them, believing
that *"when pieces of clothing that had touched Paul's
body were laid upon the sick, they were healed and the
demons had to flee!"* People reached for the hem of my
garment and were healed because of their faith level!
The same Holy Spirit power heals today as healed
through Jesus and Paul.

As we went back to the hotel, there was a holy hush
which fell on us and we all said the same thing, "Not one
of us will ever be the same because of the glory of God
that we saw in Bogota." It has done something to all the
evangelistic team that words cannot express.

The power of God exhibited in Bogota has made us
shrink into oblivion as we stand in awe at the wonder of
His majesty, glory and grace! You cannot stand in the
Presence of the Almighty God and see His wondrous
handiwork and be the same person you were when you
came. And we don't want to be!

Our son-in-law, Bob Barker said, "They came with
the most horrible diseases we've ever seen, but they
didn't take them home with them!"

It is almost like little firecrackers are being set off in
many, many areas, and as several of these are set in place,
they become as powerful as sticks of dynamite. As one is
set off, there is a chain reaction that sets off the next and
the next and the next - and tomorrow or the next day or
the next the whole world will hear the *"explosion"*, the
message of Miracle Healing Evangelism that is spreading rapidly around the world!

Manoel Ferrera came, he watched and he learned how he could be instrumental in supplying this key, this simple tool which could make supernatural evangelists out of all thirteen million of his people - thirteen million all doing the works of Jesus at one time!

He wept as he saw some eight to ten thousand receive the baptism with the Holy Spirit during the two Sunday services.

He wept as he saw over a hundred people jump out of wheelchairs or drop their crutches and walk out onto the coliseum floor praising God. He had never seen the likes of this powerful manifestation of Jesus' healing touch.

He received! He heard the warning! He heard the trumpet! He is now in Brazil preparing to do a quick work to train all THIRTEEN MILLION church members as well as the new additions to the kingdom of God they will make daily.

We challenged him to let us help him do the greatest miracle ever seen on earth. We knew in our hearts God told us this can be done.

Over eighteen months ago, God put into our hearts the vision that He wanted to set an example before the world the swiftness with which He can reach all the world. He put on our hearts to train every one of the thirteen million Assemblies of God members in Brazil how to perform the Great Commission in total, ALL OF IT!

Impossible? NO!! Not with God when we hear the announcement that Jesus is coming soon!

We believe God has sent a word to us to tell the body of Christ what He plans to do to reach the five billion people of the world to tell them about Jesus.

When we left Bogota, we praised God and told Him that if we never stood in His glory again, we knew we had here because of what had happened. He had truly shown us "great and mighty things that we knew not of."

The next day we went over the mountains to Cali,
Colombia. Word had gotten to Cali before we did, telling
of the wonderful miracles that happened in Bogota, and
they were ready for a real *explosion!*

The crowd was so excited that they were almost impossible to control, even with the armed guards who pa-
troled the arena. There was a soccer game the same night,
so many people thought there would be a small attendance, but the stands were crowded with people who believed God for healings! The news of signs and wonders
spread quickly, and the press of the crowd was beyond
anything we could ever imagine.

We could hardly wait to go down to the wheelchair
section because our faith was at such a high level, we
knew God would perform miracles again. But word came
to us that the police would not let us off of the stage because of the danger to us. The people were so hungry for
God, the police felt they would stampede and we would
be "killed" in the press of the crowd.

Our hearts cried out. We wanted so badly to go down
there and lay hands on the sick when we heard the small
voice of God over the enthusiastic praise and worship.
He said, "What did I send you to Colombia to do?"

We said, "Thank You, Father. You sent us down here
to teach these people that if Charles and Frances can do
it, they can do it, too!" God had given us one night of real
glory and then He reminded us in the most simple way
that He wanted the ordinary believers who had been
trained to know what they could actually accomplish in
the name of Jesus and by the power of the Holy Spirit!

When the two of us laid hands on the people in the
wheelchairs in Bogota, only one person came out at a

time, but what happens when possibly 500 people lay hands on the cripples at one time? We were soon to find out.

We explained that the healing teams had been trained and could do exactly the same things that we could. We asked those on the healing teams to go to the wheelchair section and when I said the words, "Silver and gold I do not have, but what I do have, I give you; In the name of Jesus Christ of Nazareth, rise up and walk" (Acts 3:6), the healing teams would lay hands on them, and they should get up and walk! We reminded them that the healing teams had the same Holy Spirit power we have, and that there is no difference in the voltage!

When the healing teams laid hands on them, people came out of wheelchairs just like they did in Bogota. They began running out to the center of the arena and for a while it looked like pandemonium. Glory to God when it is caused by the power of God. The first one who came out of a wheelchair was a paraplegic. He ran to the center of the arena and began twirling around in the center of the arena floor. His picture appeared on the front page of the paper the next morning! It was proof that "if Charles and Frances can do it, you can do it, too!"

When the call for the baptism with the Holy Spirit was made, over 6,000 came and it was a real night of Pentecost. Most of them who received the Holy Spirit had just gotten saved, because 95% of them raised their hands that they had prayed the sinner's prayer for the first time.

Signs and wonders will always be followed by a great harvest of souls!

This word that was so vividly and clearly placed into our hearts in early November, 1986, came to our remembrance:

"Thus far in 1986 I have set the foundation. During the last two months of 1986 I will put the dynamite in place. During the first four months of 1987, I will set off an explosion which will go around the world, and THEN..."

We have heard loudly and clearly what the *"AND THEN..."* means. Jesus made it clear that every creature, all five billion of the population of the earth, will hear the gospel from ordinary believers with signs and wonders following.

We heard Jesus say that these new believers will become miracle-working disciples.

We heard Jesus say that every one of these believers and the ones they win to Jesus will be endued with the power of the Holy Spirit, will speak in tongues and will be a witness by doing the supernatural with signs and wonders following.

If we went to Bogota, and saw the miraculous, and then nothing happened after we left, we would have gone in vain. Yes, it's wonderful to see bodies healed by the power of God, but what thrills us is that they are continuing what was started there.

Ray Vincent, missionary of the Foursquare Church in Bogota, Colombia, recently called our office. He shared with us about the exciting meetings that were continuing to occur regularly in Bogota since our Healing Explosion in that city one year ago.

"The video healing tapes have changed our ministry. We are now planning Healing Explosions in many places," he explained. "Can you imagine a Healing Explosion in the jungles of Peru?" They will do the training with the audio portion of the healing tapes.

They are anticipating visiting several other cities as well as some of the Caribbean Islands with the healing message within the next year.

Jaime Roman, one of our interpreters at our Colombia meetings, confirmed the miracles were continuing when he described an "explosion" they had held.

"A nine-year-old boy was born blind - he saw for the first time.

"A deaf-mute was healed.

"A young boy was very short for his age and wanted to grow to normal height. He left praising God for his added three inches in height.

"Many who came in wheelchairs were healed and walking by the end of the meeting."

This is but one example of where our Mission Outreach is successfully turning sickness into health, death into life, unbelievers into "miracle-workers" and "pew-warmers" into active "power-packed" Christians.

We have heard the trumpet! We have heard the announcement of Jesus that He is coming soon and we Christians must prepare for His coming!

We have opened our minds and hearts to perform the impossible. We believe God is doing a new thing on earth and we believe it will be done quickly!

One time God gave a brief prophecy during a Miracle Service. He simply said, *"What I have said, I will perform!"*

We plan to perform all God tells us, and we hear the trumpet which has already been blown!

Chapter Three

THE MIRACLE OF MANILA

by Frances

Just one month from the time we went to Bogota, Colombia, we left for the Philippines.

Where do you start when a story has so many fabulous parts? Manila was exciting from the word "go". When we arrived in San Francisco, we called our office to see if anything critical had come in since we left, because we knew we would not be in touch with them for a week. The great news we received was that there had been a coup in the Philippines and that the Christian television station had been taken over by the enemy!

Of course, stories are always blown up but it was a moment of decision - do we go to the Philippines in the face of machine guns? We checked with the Philippine Airlines and they encouraged us to go because they felt the story was blown out of proportion.

We talked with the other members of the team and no one wanted to retreat. We were all in the mood to advance. So it was a miracle that not even one person showed any signs of wanting to remain in the U.S. and not go on the trip.

The trip over was a beautiful flight and when we arrived in Manila, the teams were ready to go. They started out the first day to go shopping since we didn't have anything scheduled until that night.

However, the teams didn't do what they thought they were going to do. When they got inside the store, they were so wound up they began talking about Jesus instead of what they were going to purchase. Before long they were laying hands on the sick instead of shopping. People in the big warehouse store were laying all over the place under the power of God. People were being saved, baptized with the Holy Spirit, and healed as the members of the team who went along with us laying hands on the sick, expecting signs and wonders to follow! They did!

They had really gotten the message of the reason we were going to the Philippines, not just a "joy" trip, but to really accomplish something and teach the Filipinos that "they could do it, too."

The results were so remarkable that the team was asked if they would come back a second day because the store owners promised that they would bring in a lot more sick people. The team returned the next day and sure enough, there were many more sick people for them to lay hands on.

So many people were healed, the store asked them a third day to please come back again because of the miraculous results that were happening there.

I went to one of the stores which had received a brochure with our picture on it. Shortly after I arrived there, one of the sales girls brought out the flier and pointed at the picture and said, "YOU?"

I said, "Yes!" They wanted to know if I would pray for a lady. I said, "Yes, I would be happy to do that." The lady had very painful arthritis and was all bent over. She was instantly healed by the power of God, the pain left and the back straightened up.

Before I knew it, there was someone else poking a finger through the curtain in the dressing room and a little voice saying, "Could you pray for me?"

I looked outside the booth and there was a lady with a huge goiter on her throat. She asked if Jesus could heal the goiter. I said, "Of course, Jesus can and He will!"

I laid hands on her and for a moment it seemed like she almost choked, then she swallowed. She swallowed a second time and there was absolutely no sign of the goiter left whatsoever. Talk about great rejoicing in the city. It was tremendous!

Next came a lady with two lumps on her breast. The faith level of the clerks was so high because they had heard a lot about the Healing Explosion that they were ready for anything. The two lumps totally disappeared the minute I put my hands on them.

There was another clerk who was pregnant. I laid hands on her for a fast delivery. Before long, they were coming up with headaches, big problems and little problems. Every sales girl except one was healed. There were approximately thirty-five people in the store. What an exciting time we had while we were shopping!

The faith of the Philippine people was incredible. They just believe that if you touch them they will be healed by the power of God. When people believe that way, miracles really happen.

They are spiritually uneducated people for the most part. Most of them have no religious training. They don't really understand the Bible or who they are in Christ and the authority we have, but their simple faith was absolutely beautiful to behold.

Everywhere we went it was exactly the same. They were rapping on our hotel door with just any excuse so we could lay hands on them. Whenever we went out the door, there were security guards, the chamber maids or other employees - everyone wanted a touch from Jesus.

Wherever we looked there were members of the U.S. healing team sharing about Jesus, and then telling the native people that they could do exactly the same thing. Many, many, many of the employees of the hotel accepted Jesus as a result of seeing the enthusiasm and the excitement of the people on the healing teams. What a witness they were for Jesus because of the joy of the Lord and their constant excitement in talking about Him, showing the Filipinos that Jesus really is alive today!

Every Healing Explosion has a different flavor. Each is distinct and each has something unique to that particular explosion.

In Colombia it was the tremendous number in wheelchairs who were healed in Bogota. In Manila we saw something totally different.

We saw a hunger in the hearts of people to actually get out and do the works of Jesus probably more than in any other city or country where we have been. The Filipinos are not noted for their aggressiveness and yet, in the area of healing and wanting to follow after Jesus, they were absolutely incredible.

The day of the Healing Explosion was a beautiful, balmy summer day. One of the most exciting things to us was that as we stood in our hotel room on the seventeenth floor, we overlooked the Rizal Memorial Coliseum where the Healing Explosion was to be held. It was really exciting because we had seen the angels high above the coliseum and here it was the day of the Explosion and the angels had come down to the level with the people who would be coming into the arena.

We saw the healing teams as they began to gather for the great event. We saw the stadium begin to fill with the 600 voice choir who came and really blessed us. As we looked down, we saw the people looking ever so tiny but marching into position and doing the things they were supposed to be doing.

Finally, it was time for the service to start. The response was absolutely tremendous as the Filipinos praised and worshiped God, singing exactly the same songs we sing in the United States.

It is amazing that wherever we go, the Spirit of God is exactly the same. People who are hungry for the things of God are also exactly the same.

A salvation message was given and the opportunity to pray the sinner's prayer. Then the call was given for the power of God in people's lives - the baptism with the Holy Spirit.

When we told them to come out of the stands onto the field for the baptism of the Holy Spirit, it was almost like a cattle stampede. We have never seen people run as fast as they did for the power of God. There was no slow walking, no poking around. The people were determined that they were going to latch onto God and the power of the Holy Spirit and let the nation become a mighty nation as far as God was concerned.

You could actually see the dust in the field rising just like a cattle stampede as they ran across the field to receive the baptism.

It is very difficult sometimes to judge the size of the crowd. However the American healing team estimated that approximately 10,000 came and received the Spirit of God in their lives.

When they started speaking in tongues, there was a sound as of a rushing mighty wind.

Our teams from America were the supervisors and did an outstanding job, but the Filipinos really thrilled us with their super aggressiveness. We watched healing after healing and person after person get out of wheelchairs. It was a thrilling sight to see the healing teams really get to work and do what they were supposed to do.

After we stayed there several hours, we went back to the hotel and looked down from our room. What a sight it was to see all those people still laying hands upon the sick! Think of the thrill to Jesus as He looks down at His end-time church.

We looked down later to see only a few people left and saw a bus drive up. We discovered later that it was filled with people from one of the outlying provinces - they had arrived four hours late. Praise God, the faithful healing teams were still there and they ministered healing. It was tremendous!

Many hours later, the healing teams finally left, the lights went out, and the angels vanished.

The first Manila Healing Explosion is over, but the power of the Holy Spirit has been planted! The healing message has begun to take root and God is bringing the increase! Truly, Manila has come alive!

Never have I ever been touched by any human interest story as much as I was touched in the Philippines.

Some people have a tremendous hunger for God and are willing to do anything and everything to satisfy that hunger or to seek a closer walk with God.

The pastor of a church in Mindanao received a letter from a friend in California encouraging him and his wife to come to the Healing Explosion in Manila. A plane ride is very expensive and their only other choice was a two-day and night trip by boat.

Much of the Philippines is poverty-stricken and most people simply do not have the finances to do the things they would like to do.

This couple's church building had been destroyed by a typhoon two years before. They rebuilt it and the next year it was again destroyed by a typhoon. They were faced with building another church building. Their hearts were deeply stirred when they heard about the new wave and what God is doing in the world today. They purposed in their hearts that somehow or other they were going to get to the Healing Explosion and take the message back to their island and their people.

They went to a pawn shop and mortgaged several things they had. It wasn't enough.

They mortgaged their wristwatches even though time is an important thing in the world today. It wasn't enough.

They looked for everything they had and after mortgaging it all, it still wasn't enough.

Then they turned to the last thing they had left. They examined their food supply for the next year. They saw three little piglets they were raising for food.

They took the piglets and sold their year's supply of food in order to get to Manila.

When they put all the money together from mortgaging all their personal belongings, they had $40 which was just enough to pay their fare one way on the boat. They finally had enough money to come.

And come they did! Full of faith and full of hope, they believed God to show them what He was really doing today and what He wanted for the island of Mindanao.

They arrived with gifts however. They brought us some beautiful dried mangos which were absolutely delicious.

They wanted to give, even though they really needed to receive. But then, that is the principle of God, isn't it?

We did not hear the story until the second day. We did not know that they didn't even have cab fare which is minimal in the Philippines - you can go anywhere for fifty cents. They couldn't even get to the meeting the first night because they had no money left, but someone heard of their plight and gave them the cab fare they needed. Someone else miraculously supplied housing and food!

Our hearts were so stirred that we took an offering for them from the American healing teams. It came to 7,000 pesos which is about $350. They rejoiced over what God had done.

As we looked at this couple and their hunger for the things of God, all Charles and I could think about was how many of us would be willing to mortgage all our earthly possessions so we could go to a meeting and find out what God's message for the hour was and take it back to our people.

Their hearts touched us.

The Philippines was a strategic point in World War II and we know it will again be a strategic point in the final spiritual world war when God is victorious over all.

Rejoice with us that there is hunger in the hearts of Philippine people for the things of God.

The miracle of multiplication went on as trained healing teams began holding their own Healing Explosions! A "spark" started a "flame" and the "flame" spread into an unquenchable "fire"!

After the Manila Healing Explosion was over, many of the United States teams stayed over to travel and minister further on some of the other islands of the

Philippines. After receiving some of the exciting reports, we almost wish we had continued on to witness the beautiful healings which occurred. However, God has given us the assignment of training the believers and then sending them onward to do His work.

A.L. and Joyce Gill went on to Baguio with a group of trained healing team members and have sent back the following report. As you read it, keep in mind that this is exactly what EVERY believer is to do. We teach, we show, we explain, we answer your questions. However, until YOU take the little "spark" of knowledge that we share with you and fan it into "flames" through practice and experience, the Great Commission is not truly fulfilled!

Since a Healing Explosion is but the start of YOUR ministry, remember that healings and miracles will follow you from that day forward. You, too, can witness and be a part of the exciting miracles of God around the world! Then we will have been successful - "exploding" or multiplying ourselves to reach thousands - millions! Hallelujah!

"After you left the Philippines, we found that God was still there! As you know Joyce and I took ten people from the United States healing teams to do a Healing Explosion in Baguio, the 'summer capital' of the Philippines and the center of psychic healers. People have traveled there from all over the world for psychic healings by the power of demon spirits.

"The Americans who traveled with us had been in one or more of the Healing Explosions in the United States and they were fantastic. They knew what God could do! They knew how to minister to the sick and how to teach others to do the same.

"In Baguio we held the training sessions at the

largest Presbyterian church in the center of town. The
first night 120 received the baptism with the Holy Spirit.
The Presbyterian pastor was just standing back watching us during the first service, but the next evening he
was joining with the others in ministering healing to
back problems and people were falling under the power
of God as he laid hands on them. The same thing happened to an Anglican priest, a District Superintendent of
another denomination and the head chaplain of the
Philippine Armed Forces. The wife of the pastor of the
Baptist church, a Methodist minister and many other
Pentecostal ministers came. We were told that there had
never been a time when so many ministers and groups
had all joined together in that city!

"All the miracles we heard about are impossible to
relate at one time! People once totally deaf received their
hearing. Cataracts were dissolved. The blind saw. An
eyeball was created as team members watched. People
who could not bend over were bending as backs were
healed and pain left. We have received reports of deaf
and dumb people who were healed, goiters that instantly
dissolved, polio victims' arms and legs grew out to normal length, a cerebral palsy victim healed. Deliverance
of mountain Indians from demon possession as they re-
nounced their beliefs.

"But it was all happening so quickly and in such
numbers that great miracles seemed almost common. A
thirty-eight-year-old lady who was blind, deaf and
dumb from birth was totally healed. An eleven-year-old
girl, blind from birth, could see.

"How can we explain it? The power of God is so
strong at a time like this that the miraculous seems natural. You see things and don't even stop to think about it.
And then later when you are back in the natural, you

think, 'Did I really see that?' Then comes the reality of seeing God at work.

"In the past we saw miracles like this happen here and there, one or two at a time when one person was praying for the sick. But now, when hundreds are praying, doing the works of Jesus, the miracles are actually too many to count.

"The last night of the training meetings, Joyce and I had told the believers that we were going to lay hands on each of them and ask God to anoint their hands with the healing power of God. The church was so packed that there was no room in the aisles for people to come forward for the anointing. People were seated in all of the side overflow areas, standing all around the inside walls, the front entry, even outside the front of the church as well as looking in the side windows.

"The lack of room was no problem for God! As the people joined hands with the person next to them across the rows as they stood in front of their seats, Joyce walked up one side and I the other just like we have seen Charles and Frances do. We simply touched the person next to the aisle and the power of God flowed from person to person through their hands. As we passed up the aisles, almost everyone of the approximately 600 who attended fell backwards into their seats under the power of God.

"We discovered from Charles' and Frances' teaching that if they can do it, we can, too!

"All week the believers in the meetings were going home to 'practice' on their family, friends, fellow students, and others with whom they worked. We began to hear testimonies of people who were being saved in the shops, in homes, and neighborhoods throughout the city. 'Miracle Evangelism' began in that city from the first night. As a believer prayed for someone in the street, or shop, or school, a crowd would gather and soon they all would be learning about Jesus, the Son of God, who is still alive today.

"There was no building available for our use in training on Saturday and at first we felt this was a real problem. But God, as usual, had a solution. The believers divided up into teams and went to the hospitals and prisons!

"Soon the exciting reports were coming back to us! They felt that about eighty percent of all the prisoners in the jails and prisons around the city got saved. Miracles happened even to hardened criminals as they learned of Jesus. Now the believers have divided themselves into other groups and they are committed to a group going back to the jails every day!

"On Sunday we held two Healing Explosions because the people were hungry for miracles. All the miracles that happened through the hands of the healing team members are impossible to relate at one time! Deaf people received their hearing. Cataracts were dissolved. People who could not bend over were bending as backs were healed and pain left.

"The whole city is talking about Jesus. The believers there are obeying Jesus when He said, *"The works that I do shall you do also"* (John 14:12). They are obeying the last eleven words Jesus spoke on the earth according to the book of Mark, *"They shall lay hands on the sick, and they shall recover."*

"The exciting thing is that the Healing Explosion is continuing in Manila and Baguio as believers are excitedly witnessing for Jesus every day.

"We remain so excited as we see the ongoing results of your teaching to many others, those precious things

God has taught you about healing the sick!"
                                                A.L. & Joyce Gill

Another group went to another area and reported some exciting signs and wonders. The coordinator for the group told us that their group went over the mountains and through the rice paddies to Olongapo to the naval base and prostitution capital of the Philippines.

The first day of ministry was to a half-way house for bar girls provided by Youth With A Mission. The Canadian team serving there had finished their study of *"How to Heal the Sick"* but couldn't attend the Explosion because they were leaving the next day for ten days in China and ten days in Hong Kong.

The team gave them an intensive demonstration on "TNT", "TLT", and "TTT". All of them needed either back, leg or arm adjustments. God climaxed the scene with a special anointing. LOOK OUT, CHINA!

She described the Filipino healing teams as very tender and deeply loving, delicate in body yet brave in spirit as they assaulted demonic spirits with a vengeance - like turning mongooses loose among cobras.

A very excited Filipino girl came rushing up to the coordinator to share that the patients in wheelchairs were coming out. She had asked one patient how she had done it. The larger Filipino "patient" replied, "I felt large arms lift me out. The strength and power of Jesus flowed through as I walked!" Who needs to "see" angels if they lift you up out of wheelchairs!

Over 2,000 attended the Olongapo Explosion with 300 serving on healing teams. Training was held at the Admiral Hotel and the Explosion at Freedom Park.

Many miracles were witnessed in this city which adjoins the huge U.S. Naval base. What excitement to see the people we trained minister healing for the first time and see God heal through them! Undeveloped fingers began writhing on a hand like a snake when bones, muscles, tendons were commanded to function in the name of Jesus. Two men walked out of wheelchairs.

One team ministered in the local hospital. A doctor accompanied the team throughout the wards and witnessed God's power at work as miracles happened before his eyes in every ward. After being ministered to, a woman, not able to speak following a stroke, shocked her family when she said, "Hallelujah!" A young man who was paralyzed from a stroke and burning with a high fever was instantly healed by the power of God. He sat up in bed, the fever was gone and his blood pressure had dropped by 20%. The next day he wanted to go home and go back to work.

Their gracious hostess said that public attendance was the best ever in Alongapo. More than just physical healing, the spirit of the people had been lifted. The mayor prayed for them as he went to the Congress and a unity among the Christians was birthed and a river began to flow in a spiritually dry depressed town.

A third group went to Cebu and demonstrated that God reigns over Cebu!

"Plaza Indepenza was the site of the Cebu Healing Explosion. Training was held in a large opensided church with 150 qualifying for their healing team ribbons. About 400 attended each night of training and many healings took place during that time.

"The evening we taught the leg thing, one group gathered around a man whose legs had been deformed by polio. He started laughing uncontrollably saying it felt like a mouse was running up and down inside the leg and he tried to grab it to stop it. God was actually healing his legs as the muscles were rippling. The man was able to then walk without a limp.

"Several of the teams led by a Catholic priest from Seattle ministered in Catholic churches in Cebu with 3,000 attending nightly. They witnessed hundreds of healings."

Menardo Jimenez, a businessman from Manila who brought a Christian television station to Manila, was very instrumental in our going to the Philippine Islands.

He gave his testimony at one of the meetings and it was a real delight. He said that even though he quit buying cigarettes when he got saved, he had a tendency to borrow one from this person, one from that person, another from his secretary and another from someone else.

One night God woke him up in the middle of the night. And this is the way God started the conversation, "Repeat after Me: If I smoke, I belong to Satan's kingdom."

Menardo said, "If I smoke, I belong to Satan's kingdom."

God said, "If I don't smoke, I belong to God's kingdom."

Menardo said, "If I don't smoke, I belong to God's kingdom." And he has not touched a cigarette from that day to this!

God deals with all of us in very unique ways and when Menardo shared that testimony, it thrilled the entire audience.

God did great things and more is to come as God changes hearts and lives within this city through believers who know how to reach out and heal the sick.

Probably the biggest miracle which occurred was that between our first and second visit to Manila, one year later, they held over fifty Healing Explosions on their own!

God is moving in the Philippines!

Chapter Four

LET'S FLY INTO
THE MORNING SUN

by Frances

Let's go in the other direction, shall we? We've been concentrating on the south and the west, so how about a trip to the east toward Europe. Let's make the first stop in Helsinki, Finland.

We had been told that the Finnish people were very cold and undemonstrative and that we should not expect them to get excited.

What a surprise we received when we walked into our first meeting which was packed out with people, standing wall-to-wall. The love of the people was so strong, both of us burst into tears immediately because of the power of the Holy Spirit. They rose to a standing ovation and we were completely overwhelmed as we saw some of the most excited and exciting people we have ever seen. A recent letter told us they were still enthusiastically clapping at every offering time because I taught them about giving to God!

The book *HOW TO HEAL THE SICK* is published in the Finnish language and they really respond to the power in prayer cloths. The first day there were probably seventy-five to one hundred items given to us for which to pray, but by the final day we had huge tables heaped up with personal items brought to us for prayer. We laid hands on each one. A beautiful woman who attended every meeting cut hundreds of prayer cloths for every service, so we laid hands on thousands of little prayer cloths for healing, salvation and other needs.

At each service we demonstrated the power in an anointed prayer cloth by laying one that we had just prayed for on a sick individual. An infected ear stopped draining and quit hurting immediately! A frozen arm was loosed when we laid the anointed prayer cloth on it.

At one service we told the story of R.W. Schambach "wearing candy" and it so touched their hearts that they started bringing candy for us to pray for, and before we left Finland, we prayed for hundreds of pounds of candy! Licorice is the favorite candy in Finland, and we never saw such mountains of candy in our entire life. The miracle reports keep coming back in!

Europe has some of the most beautiful churches in the entire world, full of marble and gorgeous stained glass windows, but empty of people! The state church in Finland is the Lutheran Church, and we rented one of the large ones for our final meetings there. This huge church could hold up to 1,200 people. The attendance board indicated only twenty-eight people attended church the previous Sunday! They told us that was the normal attendance, but word had already gone through the town about our miracle service! One hour before starting time they closed the church and bolted the door. Fourteen hundred people had jammed themselves on the inside. Their excitement was tremendous and they were fervent in their prayers wanting God to move in their midst.

A well-known drunk got saved and immediately delivered from alcohol. He was totally "spaced out" when he came forward, but with salvation came an instant sobering up! This was a sign and a wonder that the Finnish people wanted to see.

A crippled man with innumerable back problems hobbled forward and was instantly healed by God. Then came a word of knowledge on deafness and approximately forty people were healed of deafness. Then it seemed there was a succession of miracles and when the service finally was over, there was great joy and rejoicing in the entire city.

It takes miracles to get a country turned toward God. Jesus said, "If I do not do the works of My Father, do not believe Me; but if I do, though you do not believe Me, believe the works..." (John 10:37-38).

According to an article in a paper given to us on Finnair, Finland has the highest suicide rate in the entire world per capita, especially among young males. After having the entire audience repeat the sinner's prayer, I had all the men under thirty-five stand and promise not to commit suicide! It created quite a stir!

Soon after we arrived a young man came to me who wanted to be on the healing team, but had not been able to complete the training, so he said, "What can I do to help?"

He was so excited about Jesus that I said, "You can be my catcher", so he stayed with me throughout all the meetings in Finland. What a wonderful job he did!

He was especially excited the last day when I asked, "Is your back hurting and are your arms about broken from catching all those people?"

He said, "No, God sent angels to strengthen my arms as I caught the people!" Praise Jesus for His tender loving kindness.

The supernatural is always there if we'll expect it, believe it and watch for it!

Two years later we went back to Finland and the woman who had cut up prayer cloths for us the last time we were there came running out to the arena floor. She almost broke my ribs because she hugged me so tightly, exclaiming, "Quitos! Quitos! Quitos!" and then came exciting Finnish exclamations which I couldn't understand. Finally I got an interpreter and then I realized why she was so excited.

She said, "Thank you, thank you, thank you for coming to Finland when I was so sick and not expected to live. I'll never forget your love as you came to my bedside and stayed with me four days and nights holding my hand." She continued, "But it almost broke my heart when the doctors told me that I wasn't going to die, and you walked over to the door, waved at me, said 'Goodbye' and then just vanished."

I told her I had not been there, but she insisted I was and there was no changing her mind. I didn't remember a vision, a dream or even being there; so could this have been another translation, a miracle of God stopping time like the time when God turned the sun back ten degrees on the sundial, and stopped the sun, moon and stars for almost twenty-four hours?

From Finland we want you to go with us to Ireland where alcoholism is probably the greatest problem. Annie Fitzgerald, creator of the fabulous "Dear God" items, invited us to come to Ireland and we were privileged to stay in her home and minister to individuals the very first day we were there.

One of the greatest highlights was that not one single person who came to the door unsaved left without knowing Jesus and receiving the baptism with the Holy Spirit! What a day of miracles!

Sometimes we wonder what a miracle really is! Is it just healing, or are other things equally miraculous? We feel there are miracles happening all the time if we will just give the credit to God for everything that happens.

Ireland, being predominantly a Catholic nation, has their churches occupied at all times with people coming in, praying, and then leaving. Annie, her mother, and friends kept someone at the church all day long, inviting them to come to her house for healing and whatever other needs they had! We had one person after another all day long, but what excitement to see their needs met!

In the evening, twenty little girls from a Catholic school came over to serenade us. They were all born again, but only one had received the baptism with the Holy Spirit. We ministered the baptism with the Holy Spirit and they ALL received. Not only did they speak in tongues, they all left the house singing in tongues as they walked down the sidewalk to their homes.

One of the little girls was very bashful and cried when we began growing out arms and legs. We taught them how to do this. The next morning her mother came over to report that she had come home and announced that she spoke in tongues and could now heal her mother's back problem. The mother held out her arms, the little girl prayed, the arms grew out and the mother's back was healed!

Three more little girls came to Annie's house the day after we left and they also received the baptism. Today these twenty little girls have their own Bible study, are out healing the sick, and some of them have had visions!

We had two teaching services during the day, and because of the obvious ignorance of most of the people concerning the Bible, we spoke on the promises of God and how to make the Word come alive! They were so hungry to learn about a personal relationship with Jesus that the response was incredible. A Christian bookstore had brought some of their books and Bibles to the meeting and they sold every Bible they had that day. Many of the people told us they had been taught that the Bible was a "dirty" book and they shouldn't read it. Our simple little teaching certainly changed their minds as they began to receive the promises of God for themselves!

Then came the evening service which was held in a "discotheque". A sign hung across a street in downtown Limerick where all the winos camp out which read, "Miracle Service, Come and Be Healed!" It certainly brought one of the most interesting and unusual congregations we've ever had! A man on the front row was smoking a cigarette and singing "Oh, How I Love Jesus!" That was a first for us! We managed to get through that and then we noticed an unusual thing occurring as we began to do miracles! Those on the back row were drinking "stout" and every time another miracle happened, they motioned to the bartender to bring another drink!

I had been warned not to say anything about drinking since it is part of their culture, but when I see the effects of alcoholism, it is hard to keep my mouth shut. So many of the people there were obviously under the influence of liquor that I asked the Holy Spirit to show me how to approach the subject, and He did!

This is what I said, "I understand your culture and I understand the customs of your country concerning beer, stout, whiskey and wine. I know your customs are different from ours in America. I want you to know that I am well aware of the differences in our customs, but the Word of God is the same, whether you read it in English or Gaelic, and it says, 'Wine is a mocker, strong drink is raging: and whosoever is deceived thereby is not wise'"

(Prov. 20:1 KJV).

That's a super strong statement to make when the drinks are free-flowing on the back benches of the meeting place! I could not say otherwise because I learned a long time ago to be a God-pleaser rather than a man-pleaser!

I could hardly believe the response. They literally ran to me asking me if they could be set free from the curse of alcohol. Old men, young men, women and even children knew they had a problem and the Holy Spirit had convicted them by the words He gave me to say!

The last man in line was an obviously prosperous man because he was well dressed and did not look like a lot of the others there. I laid hands on him and he fell under the power on a sticky, beer-soaked floor. He had literally sucked the power of God right out of me when he fell. He stood up, brushed himself off, grabbed me and said, "Shure and begorra, I'll believe I'm delivered if you'll kiss me, lass!"

I remembered what Paul said, "I have become ALL things to ALL men, that I might by all means save some" (I Cor 9:22). And you're right! I planted a kiss on his cheek and he got saved! Glory!

Never a dull moment in the life of a miracle-working believer!

We had ridden the train between Dublin and Limerick and had a wonderful time eating an "Irish" breakfast and looking at the beautiful meadows, spotted with black and white cows! We were rejoicing about some of the miraculous things that happened in our service there. We have discovered that people are the same all over the world, whether they're black, white, yellow or red. They're hungry for a living God, but their reactions when they see Jesus alive and well is sometimes surprising and certainly totally different from what you may have seen in your own country.

Probably the most shocking thing to us was a woman, heavily under the influence of drugs, who came to our service. It was extremely difficult to minister to her because she was literally "out of it" and at that time we did not actually see any immediate results. However, she came back that night, full of vim, vigor and vitality, and shared her exciting testimony.

Rather than tell it to you, here are her own words: "I had about given up that anything good could ever happen to me again. I had suffered excruciating pain for four years and had been unable to do anything for myself or family. *I could not even lift up a cup of coffee.*

"On the day of your miracle service, I went to the hospital for treatment and drugs to keep the pain out of my body for a little while. I came home and had to be put to bed because I felt so terrible.

"I had heard about your meeting and told my sister that I felt I just had to go because I knew I could get healed. She brought me but I was so doped up I hardly knew what was going on. You called out a word of knowledge and I came up and you laid hands on me, but I couldn't tell anything had happened because I was so under the influence of the medication.

"By that afternoon the drugs had worn off and I realized I HAD BEEN HEALED! When my children came home from school, they could hardly believe what had happened to their mother.

"I even did a height kick for them and they went all over the neighborhood telling everyone what had happened. I came back to the Full Gospel meeting that night and did height kicks all over the place.

"God is really fabulous, because I am totally

healed!"

I asked her what a height kick was, and she demonstrated by standing still and kicking one leg straight
up! We have a picture taken with her leg in mid-air!

Nothing should surprise us with God!

Dublin was no exception! It was full of surprises and
new things! A group of young drug addicts heard that a
church was serving a free lunch so they decided to come
and sit in on the meeting and get warm because the
weather was one of those real "biting" cold days. The
church wasn't much warmer, but it was still better than
being on the outside.

As they began to watch the simple miracles of arms
and legs growing out they became totally changed individuals! They had never seen anything like that in their
entire life, and as the signs and wonders continued, they
decided they wanted this same Jesus who was so alive He
was doing these supernatural things! They were set free
from drugs, and as soon as they had enjoyed their free
lunch, they went out onto the streets for a little while. We
wondered if they would be back, and it didn't take us
long to find out why they had left the church.

These new babies in Christ get the message so fast it
makes your head swim. They had gone out on the streets
and told the people who were walking up and down that
we were "dancing" in the church. We had taken some
time during the morning service to teach on praise from
the 150th Psalm. We had just started the afternoon
praise and worship when the boys returned with their
"catch". Charles was praising God in the dance when a
real old lady came up to him, hooked her arm in his and
said, "It's been a long time since I've been to a dance!"
She didn't know what kind of a "dance" she was getting
herself into, but before she got out she got saved, healed

and baptized with the Holy Spirit! Glory!

What's your impression of Holland? Most of us think of wooden shoes and tulips. While they have both of those things there, the wooden shoes are for tourists to take home and fill with artificial flowers, and the tulips are just as beautiful and plenteous as you could imagine.

There is more than that to the country of Holland.

On our first night in Holland, we attended communion at the Kom en Zie (Come and See) Church and experienced one of the most remarkable services of our entire life. After praise and worship, spontaneous testimonies began to come forth from the congregation.

Jesus said, "Do this in remembrance of Me." What do you think of when you remember Jesus? I always think of what He did for me. How He saved me, baptized me with the Holy Spirit, gave me a love, joy and happiness that I had never known in my entire life. Gave me a life that is so thrilling and exciting that I can never thank Him enough. I have always felt that communion should be a time of remembering all the wonderful things Jesus did for us.

Suddenly we found ourselves sitting in a congregation that had the same feeling. An ex-drug addict jumped up and emotionally said, "I thank God for saving me and delivering me from drugs and giving me a peace I'd never known."

Immediately, another individual jumped up and gave a heart-stirring testimony. Even though we could not understand one word of Dutch, we wept Holy Spirit tears because of the anointing of God on the service. When the interpreter gave us the message, we already knew in the Spirit what was transpiring.

There were probably thirty-five testimonies given

before the actual communion was taken. This is the way we should remember Jesus!

We had never experienced a communion service like this one so we came home and had one at our church and one at the Greater Life Christian Center in Dallas (Bob and Joan's church). The results were phenomenal! At each service many individuals said it was the most powerful service they had ever seen. A woman gave a moving testimony which stirred the hearts of many people. She said, "I did not love my husband, and I asked Jesus to give me a supernatural love for him because I knew I should love him." She wept as she said, "Jesus flooded my soul with a love for my husband. He bathed me with so much love I could hardly stand it as He supernaturally gave me a love I had never known for my husband!"

Another couple came up and gave an exciting testimony. She had been an epileptic and told never to have children. She came to a miracle service and was healed when we cast out the spirit of epilepsy. She has never had a seizure since then.

They came to another service and asked God for a baby. We laid hands on them and less than a year later God gave them a healthy, normal little girl! What a joy it was to dedicate her to the Lord! Their testimony touched people who had the same problems!

Is Communion Intoxicated?
by Charles

One day as we were riding along a highway through a forest of beautiful fall colored trees, I was thinking to God and Jesus and received a very interesting answer to a question which arose in my mind.

"Father," I thought, "the Old Testament is full of references to 'first' - first fruit, first sons etc., and Jesus was the firstborn from the dead (Revelation 1:5). Almost all scriptures have a spiritual meaning in physical examples, so what was the spiritual significance of turning water into wine as Jesus' FIRST MIRACLE?"

His instant reply to my question was, "Think of communion." Bread was eaten symbolically in remembrance of His body and wine as symbolic of His blood. Then John, chapter three, came to my mind.

"Most assuredly, I say to you, unless one is born again, he cannot see the kingdom of God...unless one is born of water and the Spirit, he cannot enter the kingdom of God. That which is born of the flesh is flesh, and that which is born of the Spirit is spirit" (John 3:3,5,6).

When we are born of water, we are born physically or by the work of our parents. However, when we are born of the Spirit, we are conceived by the Holy Spirit and born of God who is our Spirit Father. My booklet "Born Again! What Do You Mean?" tells much about this.

The "first" thing we must do to enter the kingdom of God is to be born-again or turned from physical to spiritual. We must be turned from "water" (physical) into wine (spiritual). Is this not why Jesus performed as His "first" miracle - turning water into wine?

Wine is the fruit of the vine. Jesus is the vine and we are the branches. Wine is symbolic of blood which is life. Jesus' blood was shed so that we could have life. His blood is so pure and holy that it cleanses us from all sin or unrighteousness.

There is nothing more pure than the blood of Jesus.

When the grape is on the vine, it is pure in its cluster; it has not been diluted; it has nothing added. If anything is added or taken away, it does not remain in its purest form. If anything is added or taken away from the blood, it is not totally pure.

"As the new wine is found in the cluster, And one says, 'Do not destroy it, For a blessing is in it'" (Isaiah 65:8).

Jesus was instituting the Lord's Supper in Matthew 26:26-29. Then He said, "For this is My blood of the new covenant, which is shed for many for the remission of sins. But I say to you, I will not drink of this *fruit of the vine* from now on until that day when I drink it new with you in My Father's kingdom."

Jesus' blood was not like the blood of animals. His was pure as was His very life. Jesus was without sin. We are born in sin because Adam sinned. His life-seed or sperm passed on the sin of man from generation to generation and when we are born of man, we have the seed of sin within us. Jesus did not have even the seed of sin. He was conceived by the Holy Spirit so His life came directly from God and not man. He was totally, absolutely, utterly holy. There was no sin in His blood.

Satan hates the blood of Jesus because it was through His death or shedding of His blood that Jesus defeated Satan. There is nothing so detested by Satan as the blood of Jesus.

Satan tried to tempt Jesus in the wilderness so He would not shed His blood for the forgiveness of our sins. Satan had been made prince of this earth and had been given dominion over the earth because of the sin of Adam. His offers to Jesus in the wilderness were genuine offers of something he had the right to give to Jesus.

"Then the devil, taking Him up on a high mountain, showed Him all the kingdoms of the world in a moment of time. And the devil said to Him, 'All this authority I will give You, and their glory; for this has been delivered to me, and I give it to whomever I wish. Therefore, if You will worship before me, all will be Yours.' And Jesus answered and said to him, 'Get behind Me, Satan! For it is written, "You shall worship the Lord your God, and Him only you shall serve"'" (Luke 4:6-8).

If Jesus would have worshipped the devil just a little bit, He could have avoided the cross. He could have avoided the agony of shedding His precious blood. Jesus knew what He had to do to accomplish the forgiveness of our sins. He had to die by shedding His blood.

Jesus resisted the temptation of the devil to miss the hardest thing He had to do, but the very thing for which He came to earth. God's whole plan for our redemption was the shedding of the pure blood of Jesus, and Satan knew that.

Hallelujah! Jesus did not fail God, even though He could have gained total authority over all the earth without shedding His blood. Satan had failed! After Jesus' death and resurrection, He was given back the authority allowed Satan when Adam sinned. "All authority has been given to Me in heaven and on earth" (Matthew 28:18). Satan still has certain liberties allowed by God, but not only did Jesus regain the authority, He gave it to us believers. "Behold, I give you the authority to trample on serpents and scorpions, and over all the power of the enemy, and nothing shall by any means hurt you" (Luke 10:19).

Satan is still resenting and hating the blood of Jesus. He would do anything to stop the cleansing power of the blood of Jesus.

Satan wanted to be like God and was thrown out of heaven like a bolt of lightning because he wanted to exalt self instead of God. As soon as he came to earth, he convinced Eve that she could be like God if she would disobey Him. Ever since then and especially since Jesus shed His blood, Satan has tried to get us to sin and keep us from being cleansed by the blood of Jesus.

Satan would like nothing more than to pollute or stain the blood of Jesus. He would have liked nothing more than to have had Jesus sin by worshipping him before He died so he could stop the blood.

Satan is very deceptive. He tries in every way to trick us into serving him by disobeying God and Jesus.

The purest substance ever on earth is the blood of Jesus.

Jesus wanted us to remember Him by symbolically taking His blood.

The fruit of the grapevine is pure. The Jews of old used it because it was pure when water was not.

The devil wants us to someway remember Jesus in this holy sacrament by perverting His blood. Pervert is defined in the dictionary: "to cause to turn from what is considered right, natural, or true; to misdirect; to lead astray; to corrupt. He in the serpent had perverted Eve. To turn to an improper use; to misuse; to change or misapply the meaning of; to misinterpret; distort; twist. To bring to a worse condition; to debase."

While we were in South Africa, God showed me a marvelous truth about perverting the symbolic blood, the wine or the fruit of the vine.

Satan's greatest tool against us is our mind. God will not control our minds against our wills. We have a free will at all times to choose right from wrong; to choose God or Satan. Satan always wants to possess or control us and our wills. He deals with our minds to try to get us to disobey God. He uses every way he can think of to take control of our minds and pervert our thinking.

The occult world is a deceiving world of mind control. You can be sure anything that allows our minds to

be controlled by mankind or the devil and his demons
is not of God. The devil has used alcohol, drugs, mind-
control such as ESP, hypnotism, witchcraft and other
such demonic controlled instruments.

What sneaky thing could the devil do to make us
think we are not controlled by such things as mentioned
above? First of all, he wants us to do just a "little bit" of
this. He wants us to sin just a "little bit". Just one trip on
LSD would be fun. Smoking one cigarette would do no
harm. Taking one drink of whiskey wouldn't hurt anyone. Having a little wine just at mealtime would be good
for you. Lies; all lies.

One drop of alcohol will make you a little drunk. The
more you drink, the drunker you will get. The more often
you drink, the more control it will have over you. There is
not a single alcoholic who did not start with a controlled
amount, so they thought.

When you are drunk, you have lost control of your
mind. That's why driving while intoxicated is against the
law. When you take one drop, you have lost the control of
a little bit of your mind, but you have also lost part of
your standards of self-control. Getting angry just a "little bit" leads to uncontrollable anger. Uncontrollable
anger leads to hate which leads to murder.

What more devious thing could Satan devise than to
pervert the blood of Jesus?

He knew he couldn't touch the blood of Jesus so he
decided to touch the symbolic blood of Jesus in the sacrament of Holy Communion. He got man to pervert what he
drank as the blood of Jesus. He perverted the grape juice
representing the pure blood by making it into wine. He
changed pure juice into fermented juice, into a mind-
control substance, into an impure substance. Alcoholic
wine! Perverted blood!

"Then the Lord spoke to Aaron, saying: 'Do not drink wine or intoxicating drink, you, nor your sons with you, when you go into the tabernacle of meeting, lest you die. It shall be a statute forever throughout your generations, that you may distinguish between the holy and unholy, and between unclean and clean'" (Leviticus 10:8,9).

We are the temple of God and we are priests in His kingdom. God said not to put intoxicating drink into His temple lest you die (spiritually, we believe) and that is an everlasting covenant.

"...but as He who called you is holy, you also be holy in all your conduct because it is written, 'Be holy, for I am holy'" (I Peter 1:15,16).

This is a time in God's calendar when He is preparing the body of Christ for the return of the Master, which we believe is to be very soon. Jesus is coming for a church without spot, wrinkle, or blemish. He is showing us that we must distinguish between the holy and unholy, between unclean and clean.

He is purifying the body so we will be ready when He comes for us. Only the holy will see God.

We were in Vanuatu in the South Pacific and the church had communion while we were there. We wanted to participate, but when the priest brought the communion cup to us, I smelled the alcohol in it and did not drink it.

All the church people from little children up were partaking because they were taught that alcohol was not wrong. When the priest finished giving the communion to the people, he took the cup and a bottle of vodka and drank it in front of the congregation. Then he filled the cup again and drank it. He was an alcoholic. One drop makes you a little drunk and he was demonstrating the evils of intoxicating drink to his people. Perverted blood of Jesus? Is communion intoxicating?

While I was practicing accounting as a CPA, we had an employee who was a reader in a certain church in Houston. He told me how he was highly privileged to get with the priests after communion because they could drink the wine which was not used by the people.

The blood of Jesus is not perverted, but Satan attempts to pervert anything holy. We believe he has deceived some members of the body of Christ to the utmost by perverting the very substance which we take as the blood of Jesus as a most holy remembrance of the one mighty sacrifice Jesus and God made to redeem us from Satan's control.

God is saying to the body of Christ to get all of our lives lined up with the Word of God and live a life holy, acceptable unto Him and be ready when He comes soon!

by Frances

In the Holland services, little Naomi fell under the power of God and laid there for about fifteen minutes. When she got up, she said, "Mommie, I saw Jesus!" Her little life will never be the same again. She described Him as standing there with His arms outstretched, loving everybody. She said He had white hair and was beautiful. The next day, she was looking at some pictures in a Bible and said, "Mommie, Jesus doesn't look like that at all!"

At this particular service, more than two hundred small children ranging from the ages of two to eleven received the baptism with the Holy Spirit. Many parents underestimate the ability of children to respond and understand the moving of the Holy Spirit. One little girl around twenty to twenty-four months was being held by her mother and sucking a pacifier. When the time came for the children to respond to the instructions for receiving, the mother grabbed the pacifier out of the child's mouth and the little girl instantly began to speak in tongues!

We had a second children's service and more than three hundred children received the baptism with the Holy Spirit at this service. God is moving among the children, so parents, BE READY!

In Africa we visited a church where children had prophesied the previous Sunday. Three children, two girls and one boy, had been moved upon by the Holy Spirit and gave a word from the Lord!

God's Word says, "And it shall come to pass afterward that I will pour out My Spirit on all flesh; Your SONS and your DAUGHTERS shall prophesy..." (Joel 3:28).

These are the days when YOUR sons and daughters will prophesy. Let us all make sure that our children are capable of prophesying in these end times. Every parent has a responsibility to their children to see that they receive the baptism with the Holy Spirit!

Revival came to Holland in a powerful way. More than 2,000 people were saved and received the baptism with the Holy Spirit; hundreds were healed and four children saw Jesus!

Pastor Cor Dusson said that Holland had not seen such a revival since T.L. Osborn was there many years ago. It was ten days of solid glory!

One of the most outstanding happenings was during the final night when we had a deliverance service. Homosexuals, drug addicts, alcoholics, lesbians and people totally bound with fear came to be delivered.

AND THEY GOT WHAT THEY CAME FOR! More than
five hundred came to the large stage on the final night.
As we took authority over the devil, it looked as though
the bones had been removed from their bodies. They all
crumpled to the floor, slain by the power of the Holy
Ghost, looking as if they had been hit with a bolt of lightning from heaven!

A pastor who brought two prisoners sent us the following information:

"I am a minister of prison in Belgium and was several times with a few ex-prisoners in your meetings. Two
of our boys have experienced a miracle in their lives. One
was an alcoholic and was totally at his end. He was just a
few days in our home and went with us to the meeting.
Just before the invitation, he disappeared suddenly, but
we found him back hidden behind some cars outside. Finally, he went back with me inside and you prayed for
him. Now he has totally changed. He isn't scared anymore. (Before that he was so scared.) And even his face is
totally changed. Praise God.

"A second man came free from prison but he still had
to pay one-third of all his fines. And that was really a lot
of money. He is jobless, and the government pays him a
little but it is too little to pay all his fines. If he couldn't
pay, he had to go back to prison. So there was almost
nothing left to spend.

"One night Frances said something about offering
and that really touched him. So he gave all he had and
there was nothing left for the entire month.

"The other day someone came to him and gave him
BF5000. That was one hundred times as much as he gave.
Jesus did this, Hallelujah! He paid some of his fines. But
God also encouraged him to trust Him for the rest of the
fines. And God went on blessing him. Normally, it is al-

most impossible for an ex-prisoner to find a job. The next day he was offered a good job. This is incredible. It is not certain at the moment, but he is believing he will get the job.

"This is Jesus. Hallelujah! "

We received a call from a man asking if he could bring his wife to the pastor's home for healing because she was in such pain she could not possibly sit through a service. We agreed and they came.

Her body was horribly crippled and she was confined to a wheelchair. Her husband and son brought her and the Holy Spirit spoke to us to minister to the husband and son first. Both of them had back problems and both of them had a short leg and short arm. We grew them out and all three of them were amazed to see God's power at work.

Then we laid hands on the woman and commanded that foul spirit to go. Her faith had been so built up when she saw the miracles in her husband and son that she had no difficulty receiving her healing. In just a few minutes she was up running around the dining room table!

Then we ministered salvation to all three of them, followed by the baptism with the Holy Spirit. What a time of rejoicing we had as this woman received freedom from pain for the first time in many, many years!

Doing miracles is an any time, anywhere event. Glory!

A single little flier brought some remarkable miracles in Holland! God has given us a message to take to the entire world to get the believers out doing what Jesus did. Holland responded beautifully!

A woman had one of these posters on the back of her bicycle to advertise the meetings. She had learned that

"If Charles and Frances can do it, I can do it, too!"

A young man from Denmark came up to her and asked, "What does that sign say?" He was speaking in English.

She replied, "It tells about miracle services in Holland at the Kom en Zie Church."

He said, "The world is terrible. There are so many problems nobody knows what to do. A group of us came down from Denmark to see if we could find the answer to life. Some of us went to Amsterdam, some went to Utrecht, and some of us have come to Rotterdam trying to find the answer to life."

The woman said, "I have the answer. His name is Jesus. He can give you peace, joy, and happiness. My husband just left me for another woman, and I have four children and no money, but I have peace, joy and happiness."

He said, "Where can I meet this man, Jesus?"

She thought, "I'll invite him to the meeting tonight. When he listens to Charles and Frances, he'll get saved and find the answer." Then she remembered what we said, "If Charles and Frances can do it, YOU can do it, too!"

She said to the man, "Repeat after me...." and she led him in a sinner's prayer. Then she said, "Now slam the door of your heart shut, lock it and throw the key away so Jesus can never get out of there." (She remembered what we had said.)

God reminded her of the next step. She explained how Jesus had died for her sins, gone to heaven and sent back the Holy Spirit to give us power to live the Christian life. The young man asked, "How do I get the Holy Spirit?"

She was tempted to ask him to the meeting, but

again she remembered about believers doing it themselves. She said, "Have you ever heard anyone speak in tongues?"

He said, "No." So she spoke in tongues. He asked, "What did you say?"

She said, "I don't know. I was just praising and worshipping God in an unknown language."

He began to argue with her and finally he said, "You weren't worshipping God, because you said to me, 'You are to take the message you have just heard to all of Denmark and through your efforts, it will spread into Russia and then down into Western Germany'". He continued, "You weren't speaking in tongues, you were speaking in Danish!"

The woman didn't know a single word of Danish, but God had supernaturally given her a language and a message for this young man. She then laid hands on him to receive the baptism. He instantly spoke in tongues! Glory!

Revival will start in Denmark as a result of this meeting and as a result of the Dutch learning that signs and wonders actually do follow all believers.

A young man named John Howard was a night club entertainer in Holland, addicted to drugs and alcohol, with no purpose in his life for living. One day he went into a bookstore and bought a "science-fiction" book entitled *THE LATE GREAT PLANET EARTH*. The book fascinated him, and he read it all the way through, only to discover that it was not a "science-fiction" book, it was the book that led him to salvation!

He promptly went out and bought himself a Bible! He literally devoured its messages and discovered that miracles happened wherever Jesus went. Then he discovered that the disciples had signs, wonders and miracles following them also!

He went to church. He was completely disappointed! He heard songs sung without much life, a few words preached, but nothing else.

He went to another church and it was a repetition of the first church. Finally he received the baptism with the Holy Spirit and began to speak in tongues. Now he knew he was all set for life and would see miracles.

To quote him, he said, "I went from church to church, but I wasn't satisfied, because I didn't see in the church what I saw in the books of Acts." He was discouraged, and then one day he saw a sign printed in Dutch which said, "Charles and Frances are bringing miracles to Holland!" The word "miracles" jumped out at him. He knew he had to attend these meetings with these people who were bringing "miracles"! He came, he saw and it turned him upside down. He did not miss a single meeting, even though he lived in Amsterdam and we were in Rotterdam. He could hardly believe what he saw the final night when we made a call for people to be delivered. A whole stage full of people fell backwards under the power of God. This was what he wanted - the signs and wonders to follow him.

As soon as he could, he came to America to find out if we had any tapes on healing. He had purchased a complete set of all the services in Holland which were done with an interpreter, but he was hungry for more. We sent him back home with a complete set of all our tapes in English. Today he has a miracle ministry of his own, with signs and wonders following as he conducts Healing Explosions in Holland!

South Africa is on the same side of the world as Holland, so why don't we take a little jaunt down there? Go with us, because it doesn't make any difference where believers go, signs and wonders will follow them and happen in any country in the entire world!

Miracles were easy to accomplish in Africa. Many people came to our meetings expecting God to do the supernatural and when you expect God to do the supernatural, He does!

A girl who had been involved in a motorcycle accident just a week before attended one of our first meetings. Her neck was in a stiff metal collar. Her skull and vertebrae at the back of her neck had been fractured. She had been told she would have to stay in this collar for a long time.

When she first had the accident, it seemed as though there was nothing seriously wrong; but before the day was over, her one entire side became paralyzed and her leg and arm drew up. This is when they discovered the fracture.

Charles laid hands on her and she fell out under the power of God and was there for a considerable length of time. When she got up, she ripped the collar off of her neck saying, "I'm going to the doctor and I am going to tell him about my healing."

She twisted her neck in every direction and every bit of pain and every bit of problem was healed by the power of God. She went to the doctor at 11:30 at night and got him out of bed to verify the healing.

We discovered there were many people who had stuttering problems in South Africa and we saw person after person healed completely of stuttering. What a joy to see their tongue released totally for the Lord!

In Empangeni there was a lady who had polio when she was a baby and had been crippled on one side all of her life. Her leg grew out and her arm grew out. She came back the next night to tell us that for the first time in all of her life she had woke up that morning without a pain.

We had a word of knowledge on ear problems one night and eight people came forward who had been born deaf in one ear. God opened every single deaf ear! What a time of rejoicing this was. These were all Zulu people.

The hungering for the baptism with the Holy Spirit is almost unbelievable. Service after service after service, it looked like half or three-quarters of the audience would come forward to receive the baptism. So many people came forward the first night in Empangeni for the baptism with the Holy Spirit that we had nobody left to pray for. We had nobody left to lay hands on for healing because they were all getting the baptism. Four thousand people receiving the baptism with the Holy Spirit is really going to shake that nation.

The first night, over one per cent of the entire population of the city of Empangeni received the baptism with the Holy Spirit. In the three nights we were there, over 2.5% of the total population of the city received the baptism with the Holy Spirit.

In Johannesburg, we were at the exciting Christian center and over four hundred came for the baptism on a Sunday morning. This was an exciting church and yet it was tremendous to see the response for the baptism with the Holy Spirit.

On our last night in Cape Town, more than two thousand came to the Lighthouse Church. Over five hundred received the baptism with the Holy Spirit. The pastor said he had never seen such a move of the Spirit in his entire life as he had seen in his church.

In Port Elizabeth, there were so many people crowded up on the stage of the town hall the last evening that we had to pray the stage wouldn't collapse under the tremendous weight. The people were jammed up on the stage to receive the baptism with the Holy Spirit.

An interesting thing happened at Port Elizabeth after we had been sharing the message of everybody getting out and doing the works of Jesus which we feel is the most critical message God has for the body of Christ today.

One young boy about nine years old met me as I came off the stage. He had a lower back problem and could hardly walk. He asked me if I would please heal him. He sat down, his leg grew out and his back was instantly healed.

The most exciting part of the story is that he got the message, "If Charles and Frances can do it, I can do it, too!" As I was laying hands on other people down the line, I turned around and saw him laying hands on a big Zulu man who stood about six foot two. That man was healed and fell under the power of God. The boy really caught the vision and continued to minister to people down the line.

As a matter of fact, in Port Elizabeth I had very little to do in the healing area because the people realized that THEY could do the same thing. What a joy to know that we left so many miracle-working disciples behind in Africa.

At the beginning of the service, one of the ushers came to Charles about an eye problem. Charles laid hands on his eyes and the man walked away saying, "Well, I know I'm going to be healed!"

Charles said, "Come back here because you are not going to be healed in the future. You're going to be healed now." He laid hands on the man's eyes a second time and asked the man, "What do you see now?"

The man said, "I see that fuzzy white stuff on the

side of your head." (Charles' hair is snow white.)

He was very excited that God had healed his eyes. We had many people healed of blindness, dyslexia and many other types of eye problems as well as other physical problems.

In Durban, the chef at the hotel accepted Jesus as his Savior and Lord after hiding behind a screen to listen to me share my testimony. Then he went on to receive the baptism and fell under the power of God. On the morning we left, two of the maids came in to ask us if we would pray for them. Signs and wonders followed us wherever we went in Africa. Both maids were healed.

Many people received heart healings. They came back to our services after we had laid hands on them for new hearts to report that the pain they had suffered for years was totally gone.

Hallelujah! Signs and wonders are for today!

Chapter Five

LET'S COME BACK
TO THE U.S.A.

by Frances

If you can catch your breath long enough after those two exciting trips to two different parts of the world, come along with us and see the signs and wonders which follow in the United States. Many people believe miracles happen just on overseas trips, but if we can get our "expecters" up, they will follow us all over our own native land.

Some of these miracles happened before the 1986 date we mentioned, but they're too good not to share with you, so we've included a few of the "old" ones (more than two years old).

What would you do if your fourteen-year-old son was dying? His parents prayed, they laid hands on him, they asked everyone they knew to pray for him, and finally called a Christian television station to marshall the efforts of the entire city to storm the gates of heaven in behalf of their son. This young man was slowly disintegrating from a healthy active teen-ager to a lifeless-looking wheelchair patient who did not have the strength to be on his feet for more than five minutes at a time.

I'm going to tell you the story exactly as it happened,

except for the fact that I did not know the above information when I first saw this young man.

Charles and I were at a meeting in Pittsburgh, Pennsylvania and as we were sharing at the beginning of the service, I could not help but notice a young man sitting at a front-row table. All I could see of him was a mop of red hair laying down on the table. During the praise and worship he never lifted his head, he never stood up, he never did anything! A few thoughts flickered through my mind. Was he a super rebellious teenager who had been dragged to the meeting? Was he sick? Was he just mad at someone?

Because I saw no response from him to anything that was done previously, nor to anything that Charles or I had said, I spoke to someone at the same table and said, "Would you mind tapping that young man on the shoulder?" The man did, and the young man lifted his head up for the first time. I saw he was a young boy probably around fourteen or fifteen years of age, so I said to him, "Honey, are you sick?"

His reply stunned me. He said, "I'm dying!"

I quickly replied, "Then you'd better get up here real fast!" He got out of his chair and walked the few steps necessary to get to the platform.

Someone shouted from his table, "He's got a cancerous tumor floating through his body!"

I laid hands on him and cursed that foul spirit of cancer, and cursed every cancer cell in his body and commanded the root and the seed to die in the name of Jesus, and he fell out under the power of God!

His mother who had brought him, ran up to the stage, and I said, "You might as well join him," and she fell under the power of God, too. Then the unusual story began to come out from various people in the room. This young man's father was a pastor. After his son had contracted this disease he had rapidly gone downhill physically. He had finished his school year in a wheelchair because he could not be on his feet more than five minutes at a time.

They had done everything they knew to do, and he progressively grew worse. Finally, in desperation, they ordered an experimental medication from the research laboratories of a university which cost $6,840.17. They did CAT scans on him for five days at a cost of $4,000 per day. The family was not wealthy, they did not have the money for this, but they were willing to do anything and sacrifice everything to get their son healed! Everything failed and he continued to deteriorate.

One Sunday night his father had a vision. In the vision he saw me call his son out of an audience to lay hands on him. He saw his son fall under the power of God and get up totally healed! The vision was so real to him that the next day he called the president of a local Christian television station to find out if they knew when we would be coming to Pittsburgh. The president told him we were in town that very night and gave him directions how to get to the meeting. They couldn't get a baby-sitter for their other children, so the father stayed home while the mother brought the son.

He was completely under the power of God for an indefinite amount of time. The audience sang a few songs, and he was still on the floor so we sang a few more. Then I finally decided to take the offering. I spent a considerable amount of time taking it because I always teach before I receive the offering.

He was still under the power!

Suddenly, he jumped up, started running across the front of the platform saying, "I feel cool, man. I feel cool!"

We certainly didn't know what he meant until his mother said, "His body temperature has been running three to four degrees above normal and he was always hot inside. He said for the first time since he got sick he feels cool! His pulse was extremely fast because of the sickness, and now his pulse is normal!" It was then she shared the father's vision with me. There was no doubt in my mind that he was completely healed!

I called his house the next day to find out how he was doing and the line was always busy. I kept trying until about six o'clock that night when I discovered he had been outside all day long painting the house with his father. This is the young man who less than twenty-four hours prior to that could not be on his feet more than five minutes without passing out!

He went back to school the next fall, made the football team and has had absolutely no recurrence of any form of the disease whatsoever. Truly we serve a wonderful God!

His healing was the kind we wish we saw all the time, because it was an instantaneous miracle! All the symptoms immediately left and I had him go with me to lay hands on the sick at the end of the service, then told him to do the same thing at his father's church the next Sunday.

To have the privilege of being a part of and watching as the miracle happens is one of the most soul-stirring things you can ever experience. There is nothing greater than seeing God move, whether it is in salvation, deliverance, the baptism with the Holy Spirit or healing. But what thrills us so much is to see the body of Christ out doing the same things today that we're doing!

The fire continues to fall whether you're down south or up north. We ministered in central Minnesota and the fire truly fell in a very interesting manner. The school where the meeting was held had no air conditioning. The temperature was between 100 and 104 degrees with no ventilation in the building. Needless to say, it was extremely hot.

Because of the tremendous heat, the crowd was not the usual size. All of the balcony seats were empty. During the service we glanced up into the balcony and saw every seat up there was filled with an angel.

When the audience came forward to receive the baptism, it was as though God released the angels who were sitting in the seats and dispatched one to every person in the audience. These were small angels who appeared to be somewhere between three and four feet tall. Each angel reminded me of the Australian koala bear because they sat on the shoulder of each individual. Each person had their own special angel hugging them and hugging them and hugging them while a tremendous message from the Lord came forth.

God said, "You may not understand what I'm talking about when you receive the baptism with fire. You may not understand why it was necessary for you to be purified with fire. You may not understand the supernatural things I am doing, but I have stationed with each one of you a special angel to help you and to guide you as you walk through these new waters which I have called you to tonight. These angels will not leave you, nor desert you because I have stationed them with you on a permanent basis," saith the Lord.

It was one of the most unusual sights I had ever seen. Each little angel was just loving the person to whom they were assigned in an unbelievable and incredible manner.

Many people saw the angels come out of the balcony and come down to minister to the people there. Not always do people see what's going on, but there was an unusual number who saw these angels ministering.

God never stops.

We went to Marquette, Michigan where we saw some of the most supernatural miracles we had seen in all of our ministry. A woman was there who had been in a mental institution for many years and had escaped three weeks previously. She was seen by two young college students as she was standing out in the lake with the water right up to her eyeballs ready to commit suicide. They rescued her and led her to the Lord, and then took her to a church. She had been on crutches for twelve years and could not walk without them. God totally healed her at the service.

She threw her crutches up in the air and gave them to the pastor of the church where someone had taken her. She had arthritis in her knees and God quickly healed her. She had several other problems, all of which God healed instantly.

Because we were preaching the message to the body of Christ that God is trying to get everyone out doing exactly the same things Jesus did, we called upon this new born baby Christian who had only been saved three weeks to heal somebody with a severe back problem. She commanded the arms to grow out. They were about two inches different in length. As the arms grew out, she began screaming and screaming and screaming, "I did it! I did it! I did it!"

How we wish the entire body of Christ could get the message that we all are to go out and do exactly the same things Jesus did! What an explosion will take place in our churches when we all understand and act on that revelation!

While eating lunch in Marquette, we were talking to two other pastors. One of the things we shared was if we would just take the new baby Christians and have a new convert class to show them they were to do nothing but go out and do the same works Jesus did, our churches would literally explode.

Did you ever notice it is the new baby who doesn't have any fear of going out and doing the Word? They have no fear of healing the sick because they haven't been conditioned to fear - they have faith and act on it. Let's think about all becoming new converts again so we will go around and do the supernatural like she did when she was first saved.

A young woman had come to our service the previous night and had been instantly healed of varicose veins. She got saved because of the miracle! It so turned her on she brought her entire unsaved family. They got saved, baptized with the Holy Spirit and delivered of cigarettes, all because of a simple miracle. That sign and wonder turned her on to go out and witness to her family and then to start healing the sick herself! That's what is happening today as people are budding forth in the ministry God called them to do.

We will never forget a certain convention in Sioux Falls, S.D. for several reasons. The first night of the convention we were in a tornado alert, so we took authority over the weather and commanded the tornados to go up into the sky and dissipate.

The next morning on a television show, the announcer said Sioux Falls had a miracle, because the tornado lifted into the sky and dissipated! Glory to God, He really answers prayer!

The next night we did not happen to hear a weather report, but when we got to the meeting, the worship had just begun when the manager of the hotel came running in and said, "Everybody to an inside wall - there is a tornado in the vicinity, and a tornado watch is on."

People ran quickly to the inside walls, and we were told to face the walls and place our hands on them. Charles immediately said this was going to be a "wailing wall" but not where we cried out for the Messiah to come because we knew He had already come, but for Him to give us divine protection from the storm. We prayed for a good thirty minutes in tongues before the "all clear" sounded, and many people received the baptism with the Holy Spirit as a result of this experience. It's amazing how fast people can want everything God has for them when they're in the middle of a crisis situation! There was no damage to the hotel, nor to the cars of any of those who were in the hotel, although the tornado dipped down and did damage property down the street.

How we praised God for His divine protection!

Miracles exploded as people began to praise God for this weather miracle. A man had been in excruciating pain for three years. The doctors wanted to cut off his arm and make a nerve block, but Jesus totally healed him and removed all the pain.

A woman with scleroderma, the disease which turns a body into stone, was instantly healed of all pain in her body.

Hundreds upon hundreds came for the baptism with the Holy Spirit as God continued to pour out His Spirit!

It always amazes us that God cares for the smallest details of our life if we are willing to obey Him. Frequently our mail has many heartbreaking letters from people who are loaded down with problems, but then there are many more which brighten up your day. Such was the letter which follows:

From Iowa..."Here's one of the many miracles which took place while you ministered in our town. A couple in their sixties have been coming to our body for a few months. In that time they were both saved and asked for the baptism with the Holy Spirit. He, however, didn't receive tongues fluently. But through you, he received that fulfillment. For two years they have not had sex. She had a bad heart. He had difficulties himself. After the healing of her heart and his release with tongues, they are proud to say they have a new and exciting marriage!"

A letter like this can also brighten your day!:

"I read your book on '*HOW TO HEAL THE SICK*'. My daughter had been diagnosed and told to wear corrective leg braces at three weeks of age. I was to take her back in one month. I was used to this because my son also had worn braces for three years. My womb was not long enough and made their legs buckle and turn in.

"I was born again and baptized in the Holy Spirit. I got to the part that said if you haven't tried this, do it now!

"I was lying on the bed and my daughter was lying beside me. I stood up and reached over and laid hands on her and said, 'In Jesus' name, legs straighten.' I felt them turn and you can imagine my scream to my husband to come and see.

"I went to church and told everyone!

"Well, it came time for her check-up. I wasn't going to take her back but I knew it was good to get confirmation. The devil made it a long ten mile trip to the doctor's office. He kept saying in my mind that she wasn't really healed. I kept saying, 'Yes, she is!' (Not knowing at that time how much authority I have in Jesus' name.)

"The doctor kept looking at his reports and x-rays and asking me her name, how to spell it etc., etc. He was trying to assume it wasn't the same child. He told me it couldn't be the same legs he had x-rayed.

"My daughter is three now and has perfect legs."

Does it just happen to certain people or certain denominations? No, signs and wonders will happen anywhere, any time! Here is another one of those little notes which also brightened our day and we want it to brighten yours:

"My foot got caught in a car door and was completely crushed. I was supposed to go and sing that night but my husband said, 'You can't go, you need to rest.' I picked up a book by the Hunters and began to read that I could be healed even of a broken bone. I was a Presbyterian and didn't even know anything about healing. I got out of bed on a swollen foot that was hurting and I began to praise the Lord with each step. The Lord began to heal my foot. The more I walked, the better it felt. It was completely healed! Praise the Lord!"

And then from Iowa came a confirmation of a miracle which happened years ago. An individual with epilepsy came for healing and we commanded the spirit of epilepsy to come out right there! That person has not had ONE spell since! God's healings last!

A lady called and told me an interesting story. Sometimes people hear about a meeting, and when they are not Spirit-filled, they are often reluctant to go because they are afraid of the unknown! However, we often notice that the kind of person who is really interested in all that God has is intrigued by the supernatural and wants to "nibble"!

This lady said, "I was a Southern Baptist last year when I attended a Miracle Service that you held as the last part of the Full Gospel Convention. I went, partly out of curiosity, but God was leading me into a deeper walk with Him!"

She continued, "You pointed at me and told me I had endometriosis - a female disease. You had a hard time saying it, but I knew God was calling me to come for healing. I wasn't even thinking of that when I came, but I had it for twelve years. I was healed instantly, completely and experienced the power of God like never before! My husband and I are now in an Assembly of God church, have been baptized with the Holy Spirit with speaking in tongues and are beginning to understand what it is to walk in and flow with the Spirit."

In Tulsa, which is considered the Jerusalem of America, we experienced a humorous miracle. A telephone call from the person involved confirmed what others saw as they left the building. I had prayed for a woman with diabetes who was exceptionally heavy. It is impossible to tell if someone is healed of a disease of that nature until they have been back to their doctor, so I advised her to stay on her insulin and whatever other medication she was on until she went back to her doctor. By the time she walked out onto the parking lot, she realized that the power of God had touched her and something was happening in her body because her slip had "slipped" around her ankles. By the time she reached home, she had lost twenty pounds just by God's power touching her body. Her visit back to her doctor confirmed the healing of the diabetes. Glory!

A miracle, sign and wonder can come in many different forms. This one happened as a result of a "specific seed" offering I had taken. God isn't limited by our needs, He can give us the very desires of our hearts if we will only take delight in Him. Your heart will thrill with mine at this exciting story which is guaranteed to give you spiritual goosepimples.

"I just talked to you by phone and as promised I'm writing to tell you the exciting and wonderful things the Lord has done for me since I attended your meetings. Glory! I'm still high on God!

"On Sunday evening, you and Charles took the first offering; you said to listen to the Lord and He would tell each person the amount they should give and to be obedient without question and He would bless us.

"I had already tithed on the money I brought with me on my trip, so I had not planned to tithe, but only to give 'seed money' during my stay. But, because of what was spoken in testimonies and then in obedience to your words, I heard the still small voice of the Lord and the amount was dropped into my spirit. As the offering was held up to the Lord, you and Charles prayed.

"You asked the Lord to bless each person and that whatever each person had asked for, that you and Charles would stand in agreement and then (here's where it gets good!!) you said, '...Charles and I believe that God will not only bless your giving but He will do it before November 30!'

"As you prayed, I lifted my gift to the Lord and said 'Father God, I want to find my sister by my mom's birthday, November 23rd and Lord, I thank you right now that You are doing it. Amen.'

"I had been searching for my sister, Terry Jean, for many, many years. We were separated as infants by adoption and I only had a picture of her at the age of two years.

"God worked many miracles!! God moves quickly! In less than two-and-one-half weeks I talked to my sister, Terry Jean, for the first time in thirty-four years. On my mom's birthday I met Terry Jean at the Kansas City airport and we embraced for the first time in thirty-four years. The joy of this hour is not expressible in words.

"You've helped to teach me to listen and be obedient in my giving and for that, may our Lord bless you both a thousand-fold return on ALL your giving.

"Much love, joy and peace in Christ," D.L.C.

Marriages can be healed through a sign and a wonder. As we were sitting here writing this book, we were reminded of a miracle that happened several years ago on a cold, snowy night in Minneapolis, Minnesota. God can do miracles in the tropics, and He can do them in the snow!

The Holy Spirit brought to our attention that there were a lot of people who needed to be delivered of cigarettes, so we had what we call a "cigarette stomp" where we let the people who want to be set free from the bondage of tobacco "stomp" on their cigarettes. Two people came from opposite sides of the stage, and met each other standing in line. None of us knew the story until later, but they had filed papers for divorce because their marriage was at an end. They said nothing while they were waiting in line, and when we laid hands on her, she fell under the power of God first. Then he was next. We laid hands on him, and he fell under the power.

She was still on the floor when he jumped up, took one look at her and said, "I've got a new wife!"

She opened her eyes and said, "I've got a new husband!"

He didn't even give her time to go back to the stands to get her coat, but he picked her up in his arms and ran out of Augsburg College yelling, "We're going on a honeymoon!"

Chapter Six

LET'S GO TO A HEALING EXPLOSION

by Frances

How about Minneapolis?

So you won't miss a single thing, let's start at the very beginning with the advance training sessions which are real life-changing to every person who attends them. The healing teams, totaling approximately 2,000, were ready for the glory of God to fall on them plus anything and everything else God had in mind! The praise started off on an extremely high plane. Praise and worship is so vital because it is the plow that makes the furrow to open hearts so people can receive God's blessings.

Then came a spine-tingling message from the Lord through Charles.

"I the Lord God have gathered into this room this night a very, very peculiar people. You see, I know what has happened on this earth for all times since I wadded it up in My hands and created it into a globe, an earth where I could hold people on it. I even made Adam and Eve. What a structure that was and when I put My Spirit in them and created all of those abilities, that was a great invention and I was well pleased," saith the Lord God.

"There has never," saith the Lord God, "in all of My creation on earth, there has never been this number brought together who were trained and ready to go out to do My work supernaturally.

"Never before upon this earth until this night has there been such a group of this type. I see you. I know each little mark upon your body. I know your hearts. I know your thoughts. I know your desires. I know why you are here. I know how I brought each of you together and ministered My Spirit upon you till I brought you to this point, but I, the Lord God say to you now, this is merely the beginning of your life.

"Just as great to Me," saith the Lord God, "as when I formed Adam and made him not afraid and saw a living being that was mighty and powerful, a brilliant likeness of My own likeness," says God. "He was the epitome of all things created. Much more beautiful than the stars, the moon, the sun, all of the things that I have made upon this earth, all the animals, the beasts, the birds of the sky, much more was the outstanding man that I had created.

"But even this night," says God, "you know that I have created a group of people to be the body of My Son and you are a great host of those people and this is just the beginning. Your life will multiply," saith God. "Each of you will multiply rapidly as you minister to others and they catch the vision. They know My heart. They know My purpose. They know My timing and as these people come in, they too will multiply for God.

"I have," saith the Lord God, "created as though it were a new reproductive system, so, as Adam and Eve could reproduce another, so it is that I have created you for that divine purpose of rapidly increasing and populating the earth with those in the likeness of you.

"Those who will do My work, yes, they will populate greatly with people on this earth but you are going to populate this earth by a reproductive system in the Spirit that will create a great and mighty host all over this earth until My glory in people will cover the earth as the water covers the sea. So saith the Lord your God."

When the presence and power of God becomes evident through praise and worship and Christians being in one accord, then a series of wonderful things can begin to happen.

A pastor came running to the platform and shared the following exciting vision which brought the more than 2,000 trainees to their feet with wild excitement:

"As we began to worship tonight I saw in the Spirit the worship go up and it was as though it went right through all of the floors and to the top of the hotel. It culminated there in the heavenlies and then like it had a command from God, it started marching as an army to the Met Center (site of the Healing Explosion). As the praise went forth it was doing battle. There were a lot of powers of darkness, there was a lot of spiritual wickedness that it had to cut through, but as we continued, it kept rising up and the continued praise kept following. As it got to the Met Center, there were angelic beings. It was the warring angel standing over the Met Center.

"That warring angel began to give direction to the praise and he began to direct it around the Met Center into various seats in the auditorium, on the floor, all around the corridors. As it appeared to me, it was like there was a spiritual cleansing of that place. As the praise continued, there was still praise coming out of here still going over there. It was like there was such an abundance that the warring angel began to direct the praise out in various directions all over the Twin Cities. We need to continue in that praise so there will be more paths cut through the spiritual wickedness that has been holding the Twin Cities in bondage."

Then I came forth with a most unique word from the Lord!

"For the last few years you have been like a baby on a bottle. You have been eating diluted food.

"But," He says, "I give it to you straight. No longer will your bottle be diluted with water. You will get it straight," saith the Lord. "No longer will you have to be on baby food which has been chewed up before it got to you. You will be able to take the strongest meat and to dissect it with your teeth.

"But," God says, "I am not sending out a powerless army. I'm not sending out an army that has been diluted, an army that has been watered down. I am sending out an army that is straight from the word 'go' and making him who has never even dreamed about being in a ministry have a ministry birthed tomorrow night at the Healing Explosion.

"I am sending you out to feed people instead of sitting there with a bottle in your mouth just drinking in, drinking in, drinking in," says the Lord.

"Now you go forth in the name of Jesus. Rays are going on to the churches that are continuing on, to the churches which are going to be making supernatural housecalls, but these rays of praise will bypass all of the churches which are going to still sit in a rut and are saying, 'That's too way out for me, I don't want to get involved.' Those rays of praise will go right straight to the churches which catch the vision."

Then came the actual night after all the training and faith-building services!

June 6, 1986 was an "explosive" evening for the Minneapolis, Minnesota area. The Bloomington Met Center, usually used for such noisy sporting events as the Minnesota North Stars hockey team, was invaded by a totally different crowd. Prepared and trained "to heal the sick", over 2,000 enthusiastic and turned-on healing team members took their places. Volunteers greeted the masses and directed traffic as the crowd pushed their way into the large auditorium to find their seats. As the parking lot filled with cars, campers and busses from hundreds of miles around, thousands more waited patiently outside to enter the arena. On and on they came - people hungering for what God had to offer during the great Minneapolis Healing Explosion.

The crowd was so receptive to the music that high praise and worship was reached within minutes of the start of the meeting. No one entered the building without feeling the power of God rush over them. Stepping into the actual arena was equally as awesome - a special "Holy Ghost" glow radiated from the over 11,000 believers singing God's praises.

After several special and powerful words from the Lord, we gave a call for salvation and the baptism with the Holy Spirit!

As the crowd cheered and clapped, approximately 5,000 people stood and streamed down to the arena floor to receive the baptism with the Holy Spirit. Quite like the cheering that frequented this busy sports arena on many other evenings, the roar was deafening! However, on this very special occasion, the one that was honored was Jesus - the Hero, the Victor, the Healer!

Charles ministered the baptism and under his instruction, they spoke in tongues. They sang in tongues. They whispered in tongues. And the power of God covered each and every one of them while photographers and cameramen from the local newspapers and TV stations scurried around shooting pictures of this momentous event in the Minneapolis area. Pastors openly wept as they admitted they had never seen anything like this in America before! Meanwhile the crowd in the stands cheered, prayed and wept as they witnessed such a mighty move of God among the body of Christ.

The healing teams were on fire and prepared to devastate the devil's work. They were strategically placed around the whole arena interspersed between others who had come for healing. At a given signal, the teams marched into place as Karen Wheaton led the crowd in a stirring "Battle Hymn of the Republic."

The power and magnitude of what God had only started in Minneapolis became vividly evident as the 2,000 plus team members took their places on the floor as well as in the wheelchair sections. Wherever you looked you could see the army of God dressed in full armor and prepared to set His people free. Those who came for healing followed the teams onto the floor and the teams were released to go to work. All the hours of training and study were put to good use as they began to minister to the thousands who had come expecting a miracle from God. Truly 2,000 new miracle working disciples were beginning a new dimension as witnesses for Jesus.

God desires to move mightily across the United States and around the world until Jesus' return.

Healing Explosions are not the end result of God's work in a city - they are but an "explosive" beginning. Those teams are now going out to spread what they learned - healing the sick, setting the captives free, bringing salvation to the lost and ministering the baptism with the Holy Spirit and making disciples of others to do the same. Ordinary believers are working in God's power to share God's best to bring thousands to Jesus through their powerful witness with signs and wonders following just as the Great Commission proclaims.

How else can we reach the lost, the unsaved, the sick? Praise God, He has replaced ignorance with knowledge of the truth, the knowledge to train others how to heal the sick, the ability to share the power of God with the body of Christ, the chance to encourage Christians to not only be faithful in attending and participating in church functions, but to get actively involved! The family of God must step out and believe what the Word says and accept their ministry. Maybe not a fulltime traveling evangelistic ministry like ours, but an equally important ministry nonetheless.

Every believer must know what God expects - the Word says, "...And these signs will follow THOSE WHO BELIEVE...they will lay hands on the sick, and they will recover" (Mark 16:17-18).

At work, at school, at home - wherever God has placed you is your ground to plow, seed, and harvest.

The testimonies on-stage and those at the breakfast are always the "proof of the pudding" that God has called the believers to walk in the supernatural. Then when these exciting things are confirmed by letters, it makes our spirits soar!

A little boy with cerebral palsy came up on the stage after healing team members laid hands on him. He was about four years old, and he kept opening and shutting his fist as he repeated over and over again "I had cerebral palsy and I couldn't straighten my arm, and I couldn't open my hand, but Jesus healed me, and now I can!" He wanted everyone in the auditorium to know what Jesus had done for him, and little as he was, he gave all the credit to Jesus!

A little boy was there who had no physical ears, not even an opening where the ear should have been. Healing teams ministered to him and when he came up on the stage, he was hearing perfectly. The ears had not formed yet, but they had started, and what was so exciting was that the hearing was there. He could hardly contain his excitement and tears!

A young lady came upon the stage holding two hearing aids. When she was a little girl about one year old, she had had a light bulb explode inside her mouth. Her hearing was utterly destroyed, but she could hear slightly with very strong hearing aids. Her jaws were wired together and she had no lips. The full-of-faith team commanded reconstructive miracles to her inner ear, nerve system and bones. After being slain in the Spirit, she could hear a whisper and could speak without restriction. She didn't even realize she wasn't wearing her glasses. God really did a supernatural job on her! Not through us, but through the healing team members who had been trained!

Another woman came up who had arthritis in her back. The healing teams did everything they could think of, but nothing seemed to work, and finally they discovered she had unforgiveness in her heart. We have learned that this can keep a lot of people from being healed, but as soon as she got rid of the unforgiveness, she was completely healed. Her face radiated joy as she realized that not only had the unforgiveness brought on the arthritis, but it had always kept her in bitterness, and now she was set free.

But the testimonies don't end with the stage testimonies, nor do they end with the Victory Breakfast. Truthfully, they should never end as we continue to do the things Jesus commanded us to do. The following letter will give you an idea of how the very life of Jesus can be operating in every believer:

"I feel like a little kid coming home with a good report card for my mother to look at. So many opportunities have presented themselves just since yesterday after the Victory Breakfast.

"I am the woman who had the broken wrist who gave the testimony at the Victory Breakfast about hearing my wrist snap into place Thursday afternoon when we were practicing 'the neck thing' on each other. I wondered and was mystified by why God gave me such a wonderful experience. I thought it was maybe so I could tell my doctor; then I thought it was so I could tell my relatives and the people at church. But it's bigger than that. It is so I can tell anyone who asks me what happened to my wrist. God knows I'm bold enough to tell anyone. How could you keep still? In thinking about it, I think the wrist was actually dislocated as well as broken and what I heard was it snapping back into place. We'll see when I go back to the doctor for my next visit, but just to let you know I'm in good shape, I'm typing this letter with full freedom of movement.

"The first thing I did Saturday afternoon was tell my neighbors who are staunch, fundamentalist RLDS people (I live in an RLDS community of fifty families) who believe that only ordained priesthood members can administer to the sick with oil. I showed them the references in the Bible, the Book of Mormon and the Doctrine and Covenants which all agree on it. There was nothing they could say.

"Then I went to the grocery store and told the store manager and his wife and two other people standing nearby about the experience.

"As I walked away, a little lady trailed after me and said she only got part of it because she had been on a nearby telephone. I tried to pass over it quickly and get on with shopping but she said, 'Well, I have a lot of things wrong that I would certainly like to get healed of.'

"My ears perked up and I said, 'You would?'

"She said, 'Yes.'

"Can you guess what I said with a gleeful grin spreading across my face? I said, 'Do you want me to pray for you?'

"She said, 'Yes.'

"So I said, 'Well, come on. Let's find a place.' I took her in the manager's office, shut the door and started from the top down. When I finished, I said, 'Now, listen, Peggy. God's miracles will stand up under a microscope. So you don't have to have any fear when you go back to see your doctor.' Then I went about my business. Praise God! I can't imagine having this crazy boldness and the joy/pleasure that comes with it.

"Since then, this cast was an opening for me to tell the story two more times that same afternoon. Once again today after church to a total stranger who was a guest and again Sunday night at 10:30 to a friend who needed prayer. It amazes me how the opportunities just present themselves right and left."

And another letter from a person who was healed there:

"When I was 22, after a slip on the ice, a trip to a chiropractor and x-rays, it was found that my back had never formed correctly. The last five bones in the spine formed almost an 'L' going off to the right. From the time of that slip on the ice, I had constant pain and occasional muscle spasms that went from my hip down to my ankle on the left side, as the muscles would try to pull the bones back into their correct position. Standing for any length of time was not pleasant as I constantly shifted from foot to foot to become comfortable. I was given back exercises by the chiropractor, which helped somewhat but I always had some pain.

"At the Healing Explosion, I went forward to be

prayed with by a team consisting of a woman and her nine-year-old son. When they sat me down and prayed with me, I could feel and see my leg grow nearly an inch! I have had to readjust car mirrors for driving, my shoes no longer are worn down because I walk and stand perfectly comfortably, and have had no back pain whatsoever since God's healing!"

And the angels were there in great numbers.

"I had the opportunity and privilege to minister on a healing team at the Minneapolis Healing Explosion on June 6th. We heard and saw many exciting things that night and at the Victory Breakfast the next morning.

"After we had been singing for several minutes, I had a vision of a huge angel leaning casually on a sword beside the left side of the stage. Do you remember the black curtains behind the stage? Well he was almost as tall as those curtains. I was so impressed with his size that I called the Met Center and asked them the height of the curtains. They said that the curtains were fifty feet in height. He was one BIG angel!

"A few minutes later as we were singing the words, 'Blow the Trumpet in Zion', I saw a similar angel on the right side of the stage, and his sword was starting to come up! Then Bob Barker started praying and thanked the Lord for the 'inhabitation of the angels' there that night."

"When he said that, I thought, 'Yes, they REALLY are here, and things are REALLY going to be happening tonight!'

"Just before Charles and Frances entered the arena, I glanced back to the stage again. I saw more warrior angels!

"On the middle of the three carpet runners that ran the whole length of the arena, there were angels lined up on its entire length and they were each facing alternate directions!

"With that vision, I knew that we did not have to worry about anything that night. It was all in God's hand, and He had it WELL in hand! Also, I recognized that it was a very important night - not just for what we as believers perceived, but as being extremely important for the fruition of God's ultimate purpose.

"Bless you for your ministry."

NOTE: During the training sessions at the Radisson Hotel South, the healing team trainees asked God to station angels around the Met Center. Several people saw the flood of angelic beings flowing en masse from the Radisson to the Met Center where the Explosion was held.

Do you have time to go to Chicago with us? It's just a little jump from Minneapolis.

Put the Windy City, the Fourth of July and 1700 turned-on believers trained to heal the sick together at the Rosemont Horizon and what have you got? Explosive dynamite!

Our First Anniversary Healing Explosion in Chicago, Illinois was primed and ready to explode in this teaming city of millions.

It started off with a powerful word from the Lord which is for you today!

"This is the hour of the emerging of My church," saith the Lord.

"The emphasis of My Spirit is upon My people and those who will train and equip My people in these days and in this hour, are those ministries that I shall exalt and bring forth," saith the Lord.

"For I desire to use My people as I have never used

My people before."

"For they are the special messengers that I shall use in these last days to bring good news to the people living in the earth. It shall not be those that propose to do it themselves. The day of those ministries is over," saith the Lord.

"I shall raise up those ministries that shall give themselves to My people, for it is the hour of the equipping of My people, for revival is imminent. The Spirit of the Lord is present. He is wanting to move through the land. And He is going to move through the church. He is going to move through the Body of the Lord," saith the Lord.

"So hear what the Spirit of God is saying, and you that are in positions of leadership and in positions of authority in the church of the Lord Jesus Christ, train the people. Let the people go for they are ready. For they desire to be used by Me," saith the Lord.

"Equip them, train them, prepare them for this is My will for this present hour," saith God.

"Now, there are those who have sought to hold My people back," saith the Lord. "There are those that have been in positions of leadership in My church that have not let My people come forth. And unless they change, I shall remove them," saith the Lord, "I shall take the anointing off their life and they shall not minister anymore.

"For this is the hour of the equipping of My church. It is My desire," saith the Lord, "to use each and every one of My people in these last days. And again I say, they that shall give themselves to the training and to the equipping of My people are they that I shall use in this final hour," saith the Lord.

"For these things that I am speaking of now have al-

ways been in My heart and in My mind. Yea, I have desired to do these things through the centuries. And I have
come to this time in My prophetic plans," saith the Lord.

"It is the time for the emerging of the body of Christ.
For it is going to take the whole of My people and the
whole of the church to do what I want done in these last
days. Should the job of evangelizing the world remain in
the hands of just the few - the world, the people, they
shall perish.

"For that reason, I shall use the whole body. Every
finger, every toe, every organ, every arm, every leg, I
shall use every cell in My church," saith the Lord.

"For this is the word of the Lord that is being spoken
in this land, and this is the word of the Lord that is being
spoken in other lands. For the prophets of God living in
other nations are delivering this same word at this very
hour," saith the Lord.

"For this is My plan for My whole church living in
the earth," saith the Lord.

"Now, the enemy will do what he can to stop what I
have planned and you need to be aware of that. You need
to be on guard. You need to watch over your own soul,"
saith the Lord. "Do not compromise. Conduct yourself in
a manner that is becoming to the child of God.

"Walk worthy of Me," saith the Lord. "And the
enemy shall not stop you from doing what I have called
you to do. He's going to fight. He's going to resist what I
have planned," saith the Lord. "But he shall not stop me.

"For even now, there is a disgust in the hearts of My
people for the enemy. And there is a disgust for the things
of the earth. There is a disgust for sin and those things of
the earth. There is a disgust for sin and those things that
have hindered My people from maturing and being all
that I have called them to be.

"People are going to lay aside those filthy rags and they are going to emerge as they have never emerged before. And there shall be a distinction between the child of God and those that are of this world," saith the Lord.

"For I shall distinguish that which belongs to Me in these latter days. So guard your heart and guard your life. Commit to prayer. Commit to My Word. Seek Me as you have never sought Me before. And I shall be more real to you than I ever have before.

"Yes, the revelation of My Spirit shall be so pronounced and so seen in your life that you shall have distinction as My child in the earth," saith the Lord."

They had come by bus from all over the city. They had joyfully ridden the elevated train across the Chicago skyline. They had driven all night by car from hundreds of miles around. They came by plane from all over the country. And they really received that word from the Lord!

The call was made for salvation and the baptism with the Holy Spirit. It was electrifying because one of the most heart-thumping times in the Healing Explosions is to see the people respond when that call is made.

The world is fed up with dead religion. They want to see a living Jesus! They are tired of being powerless - they want the power of God in their lives!

More than 4,500 responded to the call, and as they came down from the stands, it looked like streams of molten lava pouring down each stairway onto the great arena floor. Pastors said they had never seen such a response to a call like this in the United States! They wept with joy as the entire arena floor filled with hungry people!

By this time, all were anxious and expectant as they

joined together for a truly "explosive" July 4th celebration of freedom.

What does freedom and July 4th have to do with healing, you ask? How does this tie together with Jesus?

If you have ever been sick, if you have ever been in bondage to habits of any kind, if you have had a loved one helplessly searching for THE answer, you can then envision the people as they streamed into the Horizon. They were searching, not for freedom of their country, but for freedom of their spirits and souls. They wanted to drop the bonds, the sickness, the pain that Satan had placed on them and their families. And what happened?

Oh, the glorious freedom they found that day!! Demon-possessed people came in the front door and went home rejoicing with a new-found freedom in Jesus Christ, speaking in tongues as tears rolled down their cheeks. The sick found true relief in Jesus' healing power working through the obedient healing teams as hands were laid on them. The love and peace and joy that was in the building during the praise and worship was glorious. I dare say that many in the audience had a difficult time standing at their seats instead of floating to the top of that great arena.

We could never document the thousands of healings that took place that day. But a few did make their way through the crowds and testified on the stage of what miracles God had done for them, not through Charles and Frances Hunter, but through the ordinary believer who had enough faith to reach out and speak healing into their bodies. Some of those testimonies follow.

A man with rheumatoid arthritis had had swelling and pain constantly for one and one-half years. He was healed, the swelling receded and all the pain was gone.

A young man was deaf in both ears since birth and

now could hear a whisper without difficulty in the noisy arena. Several others also reported improvement in their hearing.

A man and a lady came who had suffered severe ringing in their ears for years. They left with the irritating ringing totally gone.

A woman had been in an auto accident and suffered a crushed heel and broken femur. Pain was gone and freedom of movement had returned to her heel.

Another lady had had a dislocated pelvis and a problem with a disc in her back. She stood with good movement in her back and no pain.

A 40-year-old woman testified to the disappearance of pain in her shoulder that had plagued her for 5 years.

A boy with a spina bifida since birth suddenly had feeling returning to his left leg, the swelling in his knee was diminishing and he was moving his toes following the readjustment (lengthening) of his foot and leg.

The Holy Spirit really blew new life into the Windy City.

It is so exciting to see people set free - free in Jesus to be a glorious testimony that Jesus does still heal today! He does care about the smallest child, the oldest grandma, the drug-ridden, the homosexual.

Everyone can be free of pain and live in divine health. We see it daily - you can, too!

We used to say, "If Charles and Frances can do it, you can do it too!" We now say, "If the healing teams can do it, we can do it too!" Some of the testimonies from the healing teams are surpassing those we receive in our meetings!

"Impossible," some say! Not with God!

"I doubt it," say others!

They haven't been to a Healing Explosion yet!

Chapter Seven

THAT WAS SO GOOD
LET'S GO TO ANOTHER ONE

For dozens of years the city of Anaheim, California has been famous for the Disneyland Amusement Park that draws literally millions through its gates weekly. Amidst the tinsel and glittering lights of the Disneyland Hotel in central California came twelve hundred wild victorious healing team members ready, willing and able to do battle against the oppression of the enemy. They had been trained in preparation for yet another anointed and powerful Healing Explosion.

For three days, the ballroom of the Disneyland Hotel rocked with the praises and cheers of God's army as they witnessed first hand as well as practiced the principles of laying hands on the sick and seeing the sick recover. California people have always been known for their boldness and gregarious personalities. This crowd was no different. There was no shyness or doubt, no question or self-consciousness.

When they were released to lay hands on someone, the person to be healed knew that the power of God was coming at them full force.

Pastors from the entire southern California area were there to participate and get involved with this dynamic end-time Miracle Evangelism. In addition, pastors and healing team members from all over the United States came to learn more, participate again and stay actively involved in what God is doing with the Christian body today.

A person actually collapsed and appeared dead at the anointing breakfast where a capacity crowd filled the ballroom to hear the "charge" and commission to the healing teams. What a witness as the teams instantly surrounded the person, ministered and brought healing. By the time the physicians reached the table, the person was recovering and returning to normalcy again.

Satan made one last attempt to discredit the power that Jesus freely gave to us and to His anointed disciples and believers. And once again, Satan lost miserably and was tread under our feet.

As the healing teams moved en masse to the great Anaheim Convention Center Arena for final preparation for the Healing Explosion, it truly looked like a massive army - God's army marching forth to the battleground.

The healing teams were in such high spirits, they immediately began to flood the arena floor, praising God in the dance as the worship began to flow through that great auditorium. People were literally sitting in the heavenlies with God and Christ Jesus as the worship continued. Suddenly there was a message in tongues and a powerful word from the Lord came:

"You are on the verge of entering into the greatest time that My church has ever known - into a supernatural era - into a supernatural dimension of My Spirit. These things have been prophesied and spoken of from the days of old.

"It's not that I have withheld My Glory. It's not that I have been slack in fulfilling My Word," saith the Spirit of God. "But there has been that needed time for preparation. And for that reason I have assembled you here," saith the Lord. "It's a time of training, it's a time of preparation. It's not a localized thing for I am doing this all over the face of the earth.

"I am gathering My people together now," saith the Lord, "for the purpose of training so that My people can move in that dimension of the Spirit - so that My people can move in that wave of glory that I shall cause to go out across the face of the earth.

"So open your spirit and be intelligent. Open your spirit and be the full-grown sons and daughters of the living God," saith the Lord. "For I shall teach thee and I shall train thee and I shall launch thee out and you shall move in the miraculous and you shall see that visitation of the Spirit that has been prophesied and spoken of from years ago - millenniums ago.

"For even in those days, the prophets saw into the future by My Spirit. They did not fully understand what I would do but they would paint their part - and another would give their part of the picture. And it all said that I, the Spirit of the Lord, was saving the best for last and that what I would do in the last days would exceed anything that I have ever done in the history of this planet. You are that body of people, you are that generation that shall see the fulfillment of all of these things.

"And so with reverence handle My Word and realize the importance of what I am doing in your life for I have given you to this generation as a sign and a wonder. And the people living in the earth shall see My glory, the glory that shall proceed the coming of the Son of man," saith the Lord.

"Elijah looked up and saw a cloud the size of a hand. I tell you this day to look at your hand for it is My hand.

And even as that cloud grew and got larger and larger, I put many hands together and yet still they are My hand.

"And the cloud came across the horizon and it got larger and larger and it opened up and poured out showers of blessings. And you are My hand and you are My cloud and you are My glory," saith the Lord. "And you will, you will be My hands. You will be My glory and they will look at you and say, 'Blessed is he who cometh in the name of the Lord.' For you are a chosen generation, a royal priesthood, a holy nation. And even as My priests could not stand because of the cloud, you will see many fall before Me because you are My cloud.

"Sickness will fall before your hands. Disease will fall before your hands. For you are My cloud and all of those in heaven are looking over the parapets at you to see what you will do with the hands that I have given you. For you bring My glory upon this place. And it will go out from here and many will say, 'I was there when we saw the glory of the Lord,'" saith the Lord.

When there is a powerful word from the Lord like that, faith really begins to build. I am always grateful that God speaks to us today, just like He did to the prophets of old.

The anticipation is gigantic once the healing teams have marched into the building, but it seems to intensify moment by moment as the meeting progresses. There is that special moment of salvation and the baptism with the Holy Spirit when the call is made for those responding to come down to the floor. Always there is that hope, that expectation, that wonder of how many will respond.

No one was disappointed, because the crowd began to flow like streams of living water onto the floor of the convention center. When the first ones reached the floor, they ran to get to the stage, because they wanted to be as close as possible, some thinking perhaps that the power would be stronger and easier to latch onto if they were close to the stage.

Over 2,500 people poured onto the floor, and they all received and spoke with other tongues, just like on the day of Pentecost!

Then it was time for the teams to take their positions, and they went forth as a mighty army, and the enemy was met and defeated. Pain left hundreds of tormented bodies. Paralysis and inability to feel and walk left as many rose out of their wheelchairs to take those first steps toward freedom.

Jesus said that every believer, without exception, would fulfill the Great Commission of the Bible as listed in the sixteenth chapter of Mark. For too long we have felt that only the "stars" could do the healing, and yet as we stand on stages and listen to the reports of the healings that are taking place on the arena floors, it is a constant reminder that "If Charles and Frances can do it, you can do it, too!" The Healing Explosion we had in Anaheim, California was exciting as we listened to the testimonies of those who came forward, thrilled because Jesus had touched them through the hands of an ordinary believer.

Just go with us on the stage and listen as person after person shares their healing. Remember, these are only a few of the "instant miracles" because many people are healed on the way home or even a week later as a result of being touched at the Healing Explosion.

A lady in her thirties testified to having had very prominent varicose veins over her lower legs for ten years. These were accompanied by pain, discomfort and swelling. One of the healing team members laid hands on her and all the pain, swelling and discomfort instantly disappeared.

A middle-aged woman with diabetes said that as a result of the disease there had been leakage in the back of her eye causing decreased and blurred vision. When a tiny healing team member spoke a new pancreas into her body, something lifted. She looked around and excitedly said, "Oh, I see that and those and these, and I see them real clear."

An elderly lady came forward with macular degeneration, where the central part of the retina has deteriorated causing loss of vision immediately in front of the person. Someone had commanded sight into the eyes and immediately her sight cleared.

A gentleman, probably in his late sixties, came to the service in a wheelchair as the result of a stroke. He had been paralyzed on the left side, and had difficulty speaking, but he came expecting to be healed. When the healing teams went to the wheelchair section they cast out the spirit of death and commanded a new brain in Jesus' name by the Spirit of God, and the man got up and walked unaided. In fact, whenever someone went to help him, he vigorously pushed them away. He walked up the stairs to the platform on his own. Like a little child, he kept indicating, "I do it, I do it!", as he was learning to walk again.

One little man flew all the way from Hawaii just to be at the Anaheim Healing Explosion. He said that from the age of seven he had been stone deaf in the left ear, and then later in life he developed nerve deafness in the right ear. The trip was to fulfill one desire, to hear again. By a command from one of the healing team members in the name of Jesus, God opened both ears. He gave the impression that he simply came to God's store to pick up a new set of hearing faculties, and they became his very own.

A small youngster whose mom was a member of the healing teams had been operated on for cancer of the brain. The child came riding in a wheelchair to which he had been confined for the past five years. He did not know the person who laid hands on his body and commanded a new brain by the Spirit of God in Jesus' name. This child came expecting God to move on his behalf, so when the healing team member laid hands on him, he responded like a tiger raring to go and get with it. He walked all over the place.

A woman about sixty years of age had numbness and loss of feeling in both lower legs and feet with a high eosinophil count (simply put, these are the cells that have to do with combatting allergic factors.) Feeling and sensation were completely restored to both feet, with the ability to stomp her feet on the floor and be able to feel it when someone ministered to her in Jesus' name.

There was a young woman with a torn cartilage in her left knee. Though scheduled for surgery, the woman came to the Anaheim Arena to be healed. Some little unknown team member spoke healing in Jesus' name. The pain disappeared. The woman was set "on fire" and climbed the stairs, stomped her foot and ran all over the place without any apparent limitations or pain.

A macho-looking motorcycle rider came to the Arena testifying of having several herniated discs caused by a motorcycle accident. He had extreme pain with very limited motion in his back. A healing team member spoke to the condition in Jesus' name. At that moment the pain left completely and he was immediately able to bend and touch his toes, and run up and down stairs with no apparent limitation or pain.

Last, but not least, there was a young man about

thirteen years of age who had been born with a cleft palate. He testified that someone on one of the teams commanded healing in the name of Jesus. As his tongue investigated the opening in the roof of his mouth, he realized the cleft palate was rapidly closing and he was healed.

Some of these might seem like "little" miracles, but if you need a "little" miracle, it can certainly be a "big" one in your eyes.

"When the seventy disciples returned, they joyfully reported to him, 'Even the demons obey us when we use your name'" (Luke 10:17 TLB). Jesus rejoiced in what these ordinary supernaturally anointed, power-filled people did in obedience to what He told them to do.

Can you imagine the rejoicing in heaven when hundreds of ordinary believers, modern-day disciples, all working in one accord, bring healing and deliverance to thousands in one night?

One of the most exciting things about the miracles shared above, is that each person who testified said, "someone" or "a little lady", or "a young man", or "a healing team member laid hands on me and I was healed." What joy that must be to Jesus and the angels of heaven. Finally after 2,000 years the body of Christ is arising in power and great glory to do the same miracles as were done by those early seventy, only thousands instead of a few!

This truly is the great harvest He said would come!

After each Healing Explosion comes a flood of letters from people whose lives have been radically changed when they discovered themselves to be a part of God's end-time army! The following letter from a pastor should encourage the heart of every pastor. Today this church has outgrown this particular building and they have already enlarged it to twice the size.

"My wife and I are still coming down off the ceiling after the Explosion in Anaheim where you told us to write you a letter and here it is.

"In November of 1983 you were in Chicago at our Regional Faith Convention. I had been asked to take the Saturday evening offering. At the last minute I was told that you (Frances) had volunteered to receive it that night. You took a 'PROVE ME' offering and for the first time I gave $1,000 to another ministry in one lump sum.

"All during that year we had been looking for a building for our church. We had been turned down by one city as they wouldn't give us a zoning variance. Another nearby town went out of its way to make sure that we couldn't move there. We even had a deal all set to rent a place in another area and the landlord backed out at the last minute. About a month before the convention we found a warehouse and were believing God for it.

"When you took the offering, we gave the $1,000 as a seed to buy and remodel the warehouse. Five months later, we had enough money to make a $40,000 down payment and sign a lease with an option to buy. Two months after this, we were able to hold our first meeting and by then we had received more than $60,000.00 for the down payment and materials to complete the renovation. By the end of 1984 we had received more than $80,000.00 above our regular offerings for the building.

"I doubt that you knew we were so blessed with that 'PROVE ME' offering. I told you how we were blessed with the gift of one-third of the land we bought.

"On Thursday night in Anaheim, you took a 'HEART'S DESIRE' offering. Frankly, I had to ask God what to ask for. You see, I know that we will have our new building very soon and a new building isn't really

my heart's desire. The Holy Spirit reminded me that I
pray every day for more and more people in The King's
Community so I gave another check for $1,000 and I am
believing that our church will double in membership by
Christmas." And it did!

Here's another explosion that happened.

Bill Schultz, pastor of Valley Christian Center
Church, San Dimas, California says:

"I was drug to the Anaheim Healing Explosion!

"Two women in our church (who are very spiritual
women) contacted me. One of them called and made an
appointment with me. She said, 'I received this tabloid in
the mail and this is what I have been wanting to do. I
have had a longing in my heart to do it. Our church must
be involved in the Southern California Healing Explosion!'"

"I said, 'We can't get involved in everything. We're
already involved in a lot. I'm not interested in "Explosions" - I've had all the explosions I need in my church
already!' I discouraged them from becoming involved.
She left that initial meeting and fasted and prayed that
God would talk to my heart.

"I walked out of my office right after my appointment with her and there was the other lady at the copy
machine - running off copies of the application for the
Hunter Healing Explosion.

"I said, 'We haven't even approved this yet!'

"She said, 'I didn't know it needed approval!'

"Anyway, those two women fasted, prayed and literally dragged me, 'They're having a pastors' meeting
and you really should go to that and see where you
should go from there.'

"I said, 'I'll be willing to do that. It's a free breakfast.

I'll go to the pastors' meeting.' I went to the pastors' meeting and the thing that really witnessed to my heart was the giving spirits you had - 'Take the books, take the tapes, train your people with these. It's not going to cost you anything. Take offerings and if God brings back in the money, then you can send it on to us for the wholesale price of the books. It's really not going to cost you anything.'

"I said, 'What have we got to lose?'

"So we signed up about 100 people from our church who went to the Anaheim Healing Explosion. They stayed at the Disneyland Hotel and went through all the training.

"It is remarkable that beginning January 1, we've started Healing Explosions of our own every Wednesday night. Wednesday night at our church is totally devoted to healing with our trained teams ministering.

"People are coming in from other churches saying, 'We've got a ribbon. Can we work on the healing teams now?'

"You have to have a healing team ribbon. We interview them and make sure they have watched the video tapes and read the book. If they haven't watched the tapes, we have another room set up with a 25 inch television and they can come in any hour of the day to watch the tapes and get the training.

"We are showing an hour of the video healing tape every Wednesday night. There is an anointing on your ministry on those tapes. We've got it blown up to a 10 foot by 10 foot screen. We worship a half hour and then show an hour of the tape - it will take 14 weeks to get through. Whatever the Holy Spirit gives me to follow, I minister and then call the healing teams forward to minister to the sick.

"Wednesday night attendance went from 30 or 40 to 200 within three weeks!"

We ran a little ad in the newspaper that we were having an Healing Explosion, but it's word of mouth mostly. People know that there is an anointing on this video course and they come to be healed, or they come to be trained to be on a healing team.

"It has totally changed my life and ministry and after 29 years of pastoring, I'm expecting to have to get a larger building for my Wednesday night services! Glory to God!

"I never took an offering at our Wednesday night services, but after hearing Frances teach on giving, I have discovered I need to give the people an opportunity to give. At times the Wednesday night offerings are larger than Sunday offerings!!"

Young and old alike get blessed.

"Thanks so much for holding the Healing Explosion in Anaheim. I'm fourteen years old. I'm so glad I qualified for the team. At first I thought it would be hard reaching the requirements and going to school at the same time - but it sure paid off!

"I also tried your 'prove me' test! I couldn't give any in your meetings, but I did when I got back home. It may seem small but I gave God five cents in my tithe bag and got $5.00 back the same day! If it works for such a little amount, I KNOW it will work for big amounts."

Wouldn't it be wonderful if we all had the faith of a young child?

"Praise God! Let me share the Anaheim Explosion with you from a twenty-one-year-old chiropractic student. First of all, I had what is called a straight neck. A woman sitting behind me knew it was hurting me and took me in the back - did the neck thing - and, praise God, I now have a curve in my neck!

"We prayed for a guy with short achilles tendons (which grew in my hand) and a muscle in his leg out of place, which went back.

"Second - a woman with adhesions and back problems, disc degeneration. Commanded new discs and she touched her toes!

"Third - a woman with kyphosis (hunchback). Commanded spirit of kyphosis to come out and her shoulder moved back in my hand."

"Praise the Lord for all His marvelous works! It is so hard not to jump up and down as I am writing you this letter - but here goes! After attending your Healing Explosion in Anaheim, California this last month, it has become more and more evident that the 'church' is getting herself ready for the coming of her 'Beloved'. Glory to God!"

A pastor touched our hearts with his letter.

"As a member of one of your healing teams, I had never experienced a more dynamic anointing as all of 1,300 members stood in one accord singing 'We're Standing on Holy Ground'. I could feel and see angelic beings in our midst.

"Our precious Lord has used me many times in the past for the healing of His people, but I must say that this day, standing with so many with one mind, one purpose, one goal - Wow! Explosive!

"As we were singing all together the people who had been ready to come through the lines must have already felt the surging of God's power flowing, the expectation level must be at the ultimate because mine was so intensified that I knew that I knew whatever disease or form of disease stood in front of me would flee! As it was, cancer of lower bowels (colon) left, eye sight (near-sightedness) restored, arthritis disappeared, left hearing restored, back (upper) pains left, TPT, TNT, and TTT was used most effectively. Even later on that night several women from Chicago came up to our room; healing from an unforgiving spirit occured as well as physical systems restored to health.

"The Lord sent me to Anaheim, California to learn and to do! So, I and my associates, who also came with me are continuing on with the teachings and the doings and seeing more and more people rise up as an army doing and speaking 'victory'.

"God bless you both as you continue on. Don't stop!"

We don't intend to stop - we're continuing on full speed ahead just as fast as we can go!

Chapter Eight

FIFTEEN
ON THE RICHTER SCALE

By Frances

From the moment we caught a glimpse of the arch in St. Louis, we knew that the St. Louis Healing Explosion was going to be tremendous. Some people call the arch "The Archway to the West", some call it "The Archway to Freedom", but whatever it was, it was an archway to an experience with Jesus that many people will never get over.

The worship was spectacular as the Exalters from the Greater Life Christian Center in Dallas, Texas brought the entire congregation into the very presence of God. No other Healing Explosion has been held where we have had so many people comment on the glorious worship as they did in St. Louis.

Rick Shelton, coordinator for the St. Louis area, gave a powerful prophecy at the very beginning which was followed by one or two other prophecies, but what he prophesied was so significant in the light of what Jesus is doing today we want you to carefully read every word of it.

"For this tonight is a wind of God that is blowing across this city," saith the Lord. "Yes, even as the people came together in one mind and one spirit and one accord on the day of Pentecost. There was a great festival in that city of many people from many different things in that city, but yet the people of God came into the center of town and began to seek My face and began to unify and stand as one people together.

"My Spirit blew into that upper room and those people were never the same. They caught the fire of the Holy Ghost and took it out to the streets where the people looked upon them and said, 'O they must be drunk, they must be drunk.' Yes, I say, they were drunk with the new wine and I tell you tonight as you have come together in one mind, one spirit and one accord even as on the day of Pentecost, I am blowing into this place tonight.

"My Spirit is settling upon this place right now, right now, right now My Spirit is settling upon this place like a cloud, like a cloud of My glory settling upon you now and you shall go out from this place tonight after the miracles take place, after the glory of God falls on this place tonight and you shall take to the streets.

"And they shall even say of you as they did on the day of Pentecost, 'They must be drunk, they must be crazy, they're foolish people.' But I tell you tonight that you are drunk. You say, 'I am so excited!' Yes, you are drunk with the new wine of the Holy Ghost this night," saith God.

"Go forth and stay filled up with the Holy Spirit and faith and I'll cause more miracles to happen out on the streets than happen in this place tonight," saith God.

After the praise and worship and teaching on how to receive a healing, the call was made for salvation and the baptism with the Holy Spirit. It is almost impossible to describe to anyone who has not attended a Healing Explosion what happens at that supercharged moment.

The skeptics wonder if anyone would be so foolish as

to expect to speak in tongues in the twentieth century. Those who are moved to respond are wondering, "Will I receive this power tonight?" The Spirit-filled believers are praying, "God, may everyone who doesn't have the power of God in their life respond to the wooing of the Holy Spirit!"

Then the applause begins because it seems as if those who have come thirsting are magnetized by a power they have never felt before to respond to the call! They all seem to get up at the same time to make their way down to the floor.

It is exciting to watch the expressions on their faces as they stand listening to the instructions on how to receive the power, but they all have the same look, "I want it, I want it!"

The most exhilarating moment to the healing teams is that emotion-packed second when the teams are called onto the floor! The twelve hundred trained believers stood up and began their march from the balcony down to the lower floor.

The entire audience rose to their feet and began to sing "Mine Eyes Have Seen the Glory of the Coming of the Lord, His Truth is Marching On" as the healing teams marched onto the Kiel Auditorium floor in a great explosion of power. Some two thousand people had responded to the call for the baptism with the Holy Spirit so the entire audience was ready for the healing teams to go to work.

Soon the stage was flooded with people reporting testimonies of healings. A man had had problems with his back for eighteen years and was gloriously healed when a believer laid hands on him. He put his faith in action by bending in all directions - regardless of how you look at it, whether bending forward or backwards, he got healed.

Deafness was healed. Another man with a back brace was healed by the power of God. A father and son healed by the power of God. A lady was healed of TMJ and wiggled her jaw just to show that she was healed. A Catholic nun arranged for her blood sister to be there - the healing power of God came on her and healed her. A young man reported he thought all these goings on were really "cool".

The healing teams had been well equipped after excellent instruction by the doctors' panel consisting of several chiropractors, a podiatrist, a dentist, a physician, a surgeon, and two pediatricians. Everyone enjoyed the knowledge that was shared by these experts. A chiropractor brought a skeleton to demonstrate why so many parts of the back get out of alignment so easily, and how the healings can be manifested by the supernatural power of God.

Pastor James Bruce, of the Hope Church in St. Louis, reminded us all that he is a very conservative person and the remarks he made were from a "conservative" viewpoint:

"When the worship service started at the Kiel Auditorium, there was something unique on the platform. I don't know how it was out in the audience, but that platform was unique from the first syllable on. The entire meeting was supernatural and unusual.

"On a Richter scale of 10, I would rate the entire Healing Explosion and training sessions 15!"

Not only was the service rated "15" on the Richter scale, the supernatural brought visions and exciting afterglow.

"I have been praising God daily for what He has done through me at the Healing Explosion. It was a totally awesome experience. Thank you for what God is doing through you, also.

"During the service as I was looking down over the auditorium floor, I didn't see any angels or a glory cloud. But, what I did see was an overwhelming sight. It was as if the entire auditorium was transformed into a huge swimming pool filled with the golden oil of the Holy Spirit!

"Our children are so overwhelmed by the change in my wife and myself that they are reading the book *HOW TO HEAL THE SICK* and are watching the video. They want to get involved for Jesus and want to participate in the next Healing Explosion.

"I am finding myself praying for the people in the office where I do consulting work and at the college where I teach. This is something I just would not have done before the Explosion. I am realizing that those people who are crossing my path have done so by the prompting of God and it is not just a coincidence."

Let's go on with some added benefits from the St. Louis Explosion:

"Last week has changed my outlook on life - from giving, which had been so planned that the joy was changed to duty, to witnessing and ministry, which is more fruitful than ever. I have been saved and Spirit-filled for ten years, but the lack of regular, visible miracles (I mean Matthew 10:8 miracles; God has always provided miraculously for us financially) has kept me from thinking I would see the church doing EVERYTHING the way Jesus did. I spiritualized my Bible reading to make it fit what I saw actually happening in my life or just didn't think about it.

"About Friday night: When we were coming down from the balcony to minister, I was almost overwhelmed by the feeling of being caught up in a river of God's power. The stream of people going down the ramps from the balcony was just like a river. At the same time, I felt like part of an army marching home from a victorious campaign, and could imagine a large men's chorus singing 'Onward Christian Soldiers'.

"One man who came to my partner and me Friday had back problems, so I did 'the pelvic thing', but he wasn't completely healed. So I did it again and the bones moved some more, but the pain still wasn't gone. I stopped to listen and the Spirit said 'sparkplug'. I'd previously been afraid of holding someone's hips, but I remembered what you said, Charles, about getting good contact so the power can flow. Instead of rushing through it again the third time, I grabbed hold and the Spirit made contact! The man's back was totally healed.

"I have been very edified by your statements about imagination, i.e. not letting it run away or getting into weird 'visions' because, before I was saved, I was involved in 'white magic' (it's all black). The improper use of imagination was at the center of everything we did, and self-exaltation was the result of it. Now I can direct the praise to Jesus and not be in fear of backsliding into what He delivered me from ten years ago. To have the person thank Jesus emphasizes to them and to myself who the Healer is."

This letter was really exciting, too! Read on...

"I have put off writing this letter long enough. I was on the healing team for St. Louis. I cannot explain to you what happened to me on the inside as a result of that experience. As we were sitting up at the top of the auditorium waiting to come down on the floor during the Healing Explosion, - the face of Jesus was outlined on the wall directly behind you two.

"It was very large. When I saw it, I wanted to make sure it was just not my imagination so I shared with others around me. They saw it, too. Some had already seen it when I shared. It was amazing how large it was and the compassion on His face. It was a sign to me that He truly was in charge of it all.

"Then we were told to come down onto the floor. As we marched down the ramps, we shouted the name of Jesus in unison, then sang, 'God's Got An Army'. It was so exciting I thought I would explode! My heart and whole being were filled with such excitement and compassion as we were waiting to come onto the floor and yet there was such a quiet awe and expectancy all at the same time.

"The Lord has allowed myself and others to minister to some at church. We have seen arms grow, legs grow, pelves rotate and people healed and rejoicing.

"God has told our pastor that He is raising up a healing center for our church. I am excited as I know that those of us who have been trained by you will be a part of this. I praise God as through this training and Explosion I have received a new boldness and confidence in stepping out for the Lord. I no longer have a fear of asking people if I can pray for them. I have approached people in restaurants and grocery stores and asked if I could lay hands on them. Some have refused but I'll keep on trying. After all, I have nothing to lose.

"I am looking forward to the next Healing Explosion with great expectation. My twelve-year-old daughter is now taking the training and will be there with me. I am so excited and am expecting great things to happen."

We always encourage the healing team members to let us know what happens to them during or after the Healing Explosion so we can share their exciting testimonies with others. This one came in the mail and shows you how a whole church is affected.

"Praise God! What a change has come into our lives! When I laid my hand on my heart in St. Louis and promised to spend twenty-two cents and write to you about what happened, I was thinking all the time, 'What will I write about? Well, the Lord will give me something!' He sure has!!

"When we got home from St. Louis, we talked with my mother-in-law until 2 a.m. Sunday morning. We found out she wasn't saved and took care of that right away. She also wanted the baptism with the Holy Spirit - she spoke in tongues! Her back was also healed as her arm grew out and she slept ALL night which for her is great!

"After our worship and singing, our pastor asked if anyone had a testimony! Hands really flew up (about nine from our church were at St. Louis). As we all spoke of what we saw and learned, our pastor said he wasn't going to teach what he had prepared because he felt led by the Spirit to have the healing teams and our elders to minister to those who needed a touch from God.

"Our church starts at 10 a.m. and the precious Lord was touching our people until noon - our entire service! Back problems, colds, cigarette habits, warts, depression and I don't know what else! But I do know different ones came back up and told how they were touched - then others will know they were, too!"

At almost every Healing Explosion, angels are seen by many or few people. The effects are always the same - life-changing!

"I personally saw the Spirit of God as a cloud laying below our elevation with angels hovering over.

"My wife and I ministered to four people with demonic spirits and they were set free. Praise the name of
Jesus! We ministered to others for healings also. I believe
the angels brought me my specialty."

At the time of writing this book, we have held 49
Healing Explosions around the world. Without exception, a host of angels hover over the great arenas or soccer fields where the Explosions are held like an um-
brella. We have been there over thirty days ahead of the
Explosions and they have been there. We believe God
sends them "fifty days" ahead for some reason unknown
to us. Then on the day of the Healing Explosion, at the
very moment the healing teams enter for final instructions, all the angels descend into the arena. We don't
know what they do, but we believe God uses them to
work with the team members in some way.

One lady reported that she was having a problem
getting someone healed and she called a supervisor (they
were identified with a blue ribbon). The man came to
help, gave instructions which she applied and the person
was healed. She then turned to thank the supervisor and
"he had vanished!"

These people are now "getting their feet wet".

"We promised you at the St. Louis Explosion that we
would write you a letter. My husband and I received so
much from the training on healing that we want to thank
you both over and over again!

"While we were there one night my husband had a
dream or vision of crossing over bridges (walking) one by
one (over water) and then there was NO bridge over the
water. He asked the Lord what this meant?

"He said, 'Now it is time for you to walk out into the

water!' My husband has been one changed man since being at your meetings. He prays for me with authority and commands the pain to GO in the name of Jesus, and it GOES!

"I have ministered to friends and plan on showing your tapes again in our home. People are hurting and desperately need help! We can never thank you enough!"

Don't neglect your children's teaching. They want to learn, too!

"Because of your teachings, your book and the Healing Explosion at the Kiel Auditorium, I will never be the same. I feel like I grew at least two feet in my 'spiritual life' - all in a few days.

"I returned home from the seminar and Healing Explosion 'super-charged' from the wonderful things the Lord had done.

"When my children saw the 'TPT', 'TNT' and 'TTT', they were ecstatic to learn how to do it too! The little six-year-old saw the older children in the family doing the 'pelvic thing' and growing out arms and wanted so badly to do that, too, that she received the baptism with the Holy Spirit and is now doing it herself.

"My twelve-year-old daughter took her new healing knowledge to school and asked a little Christian friend if she would like to have her pelvic bones rotated. Since it was recess time, Jesus ended up with a captive audience. Some comments given to Angie were: 'Wow, I wish I could be like you!' 'You're lucky!' 'I wish I were you!' etc.

"Angie told her friends, 'It's Jesus that you really want to be like. Through Him and the Holy Ghost baptism, you can do this, too!' Today there are several new members of the kingdom of God (also baptized with the

Holy Spirit) at Angie's school because of the precious healing power God allows us to use to glorify Him."

The following is an exciting testimony from a man from O'Fallon, Missouri. He shares what God has done for him; however he has also included documentation from his personal physician as proof to the world that indeed God does heal today!

"I give this testimony in the name of Jesus and to His glory!

"Sunday, we had Charles and Frances Hunter as guests at Church on the Rock. I watched many miracles take place right before my eyes. I saw a doctor examine each healing before and after prayer. God had arranged the opportunity for me to be only about six feet away, on the platform in the choir. I could sense God stimulating my faith to believe He heals people today. I also knew the pain I'd learned to tolerate was not normal and healthy. Just sitting there quietly, I didn't tell anyone about my need. When the service was over, I had an attack from the enemy, feeling I'd lost my chance to be healed. At that very moment, God spoke to my heart. He said, 'Ron, come tomorrow night and I will heal your back.'

"That night, I had the doctor examine my back. He agreed with the fact that I needed a definite miracle. I confessed to him, 'God's going to heal my back tomorrow night!'

"I really began to get excited. For the first time in my Christian walk, I knew and was expecting God to heal my back.

"I remembered the many times over the years when I hurt so bad I could barely walk. I would grit my teeth just to pick up my children when they were little.

"Injured falling off a horse twenty-five years ago, I saw many doctors and chiropractors, and spent a lot of money. Finally, I gave up and decided to live with the pain. After a while, I got used to the pain. It was just numb all the time.

"When I got home, I could not sleep. I just laid awake talking to the Lord. As I lay there, God's voice reminded me of old x-rays I had taken in 1980 of my full back.

"I understood that some people don't believe God wants them healed and healthy. Or that He does do miracles today. My x-rays would be undeniable proof of God's healing power in people today.

"Monday night, I took my x-rays with me to church. I believed God would call me out when it was the right time. Very soon after the singing, the moment God had promised came. Frances Hunter looked straight at me and called me up onto the platform.

"According to God's Word, the three on the healing team laid their hands on me and began to pray. I believe God did it that way to show everyone the healing was from Him through anyone, not just the evangelists.

"Immediately, I knew something had happened inside my body. The doctor examined my back and confirmed the spine was in perfect alignment. To dispel all doubt and question, I had a second x-ray taken.

"The x-rays revealed God's perfection in His healing power. My back is completely healed. God kept His promise and healed me!

"All the praise, all the honor, all the glory goes to my miracle-working God.

"Above all, know this - what He did for me, He will do for you!"

And to that we say a big AMEN! He'll do it for YOU!

Chapter Nine

BLOW THE TRUMPET IN ZION

Angels blowing trumpets lined the roof of the great First Assembly of God Church in Fargo on August 8, 1986, calling people in from the north, the east, the south and the west! What a sight to behold as we left the freeway and caught sight of the building!

God spoke and said, "By My Spirit, I am causing the sound of these trumpets to be heard all across this area, wooing people to come to the Healing Explosion."

Each day as we drove to the church, the angels were very apparent. Even on the Sunday afternoon of the Explosion, they were still there at 2:30 p.m. calling them to the meeting.

What a thrill it was when Pastor Curt Frankhauser shared at the Victory Banquet that this was a real confirmation to him. At their prayer meeting two weeks prior to the Healing Explosion, they had all faced different directions and began calling people in from specific towns within a three hundred mile radius!

God confirms His Word!

The Spirit really drew them, because after parking their cars, they walked for blocks to reach the Healing Explosion in Fargo, North Dakota. And their walk was not in vain. Some 450 healing team members were waiting with excitement to lay their hands on the sick and see them recover. Their faith was at a red-hot level and they could hardly wait until the sick lined up in front of them.

A four-year-old came with a large umbilical hernia. It did not respond the first time hands were laid on it, but when the healing team member continued to command the muscles to go into place, the hernia went back in and was completely healed!

A lady who was totally deaf in her right ear gave away her hearing aid as God totally restored her hearing.

A young girl was healed of scoliosis and her back appeared perfectly straight after a healing team had commanded the spirit of scoliosis to come out. About fifteen different people were healed of scoliosis! This is what one healing will do - it will spark the faith of others with the same problem to receive a healing themselves!

A young girl who was a long distance runner had problems with her feet and legs. She was discouraged when she was told she would have to stop running. She was healed and left the stage *running* without difficulty.

A little girl with no arches was healed. Many cases of arthritis were instantly healed and people reported the pain was gone. Many were bending, stretching and twisting to show they had no pain.

Hundreds of back and neck problems were healed.

At the Victory Banquet on Sunday night following the Healing Explosion, the testimonies were super exciting as the people shared what God had done.

One woman said that since her husband had died and her children were all married and living away from home, she felt she had no purpose in life. But NOW she knew she had a purpose - to go out and fulfill the Great Commission and lay hands on the sick, minister salvation, the baptism with the Holy Spirit and deliverance!

If there is anything we want to convey to the body of

Christ, it is to be up-to-date with what God is doing today. They came from France, Germany, Japan, Colombia, Mexico, Belize and Canada to take the Jesus' message via the video tapes and books back to their countries.

People are contacting us everywhere we go, asking us to bring Healing Explosions to different foreign countries. One pastor from the Philippines said he was going to take all the materials back and hold a Healing Explosion there himself! Praise Jesus, this is what God is saying to the body of Christ! Step out and fulfill the Great Commission!

Exciting letters always follow Healing Explosions, and we picked out these two to bless you before we move south to Tampa, Florida.

"Just a note to let you know I am seeing so much better since attending the Fargo Healing Explosion. Thank you ever so much for coming to the north country!

"I could not see to drive or read (or write either) because of cataracts caused by iritis. Surgery wouldn't help because of the 'chronic inflamation' - and we had no money for surgery anyway.

"I didn't notice any change in vision at the service, but when we stopped at a fast food restaurant on the way home, I realized I could read their menu sign which hung behind the counter. I hadn't been able to do that for months. On the eye chart, I couldn't read the top E. My husband and I called my parents right away and we rejoiced over the phone. I suggested to my husband that we go to a different restaurant every day so I could read the menu to him! But he suggested I just read the cookbook instead! (This guy has no sense of celebration!!)

"When I bought your books at the Fargo service, I couldn't see the print, but NOW I CAN!!

"There have been many healings on our reservation since we saw your video tapes. My husband is a native American Indian and pastors a church on Leech Lake Reservation."

We always get excited when someone's faith is increased as they minister healing:

"One lady had pain so excruciating in the heel of her foot, the doctor told her maybe she cracked her heel sometime or other. He did not know what to do for it. We did the leg thing and the pelvic thing. The pain immediately went as she walked on it.

"Thank you! We feel that our own faith has grown leaps and bounds in the healing area!"

It's getting cool up north, so let's go south for an explosion! How about Florida? This will give you a bird's eye view of what happened there! This story was so beautifully written, we're giving you all of it. Maybe you can put yourself into this woman's shoes as she saw, felt and experienced a Healing Explosion!

"Tampa - Home of the Tampa Bay Buccaneers, the resort and visitor hub of Florida's west coast. I found myself at the Tampa State Fairgrounds, site of the yearly Florida State Fair. The buildings usually house homemade cookies, candies and clothes, home-grown vegetables and fruits, pigs, chickens, cattle, horses and thousands upon thousands of hopeful entrants with dreams of 'blue' ribbons...or even 'purple' ribbons indicating the 'best' in the state!

"Outside venders shout their wares, delicious smells waft their way through the night breezes calling and advertising the many offerings of delicacies to tempt your palate. Old, young, strong, weak, men, women and children walk and wander in amazement at the sights, the sounds, the smells, the rides, the games of chance, the sparkling lights that gather at the Tampa State Fairgrounds during 'Fair Week'.

"November 15, 1986, brought quite another group. Oh, there were the old, the young, the weak and the strong. Men, women and children came. With great expectation and anticipation, people streamed into the Fairground parking lot over a period of four hours and made their way through the cars and down the walks to that large building which normally held horse and cattle shows.

"Out of the open doors came the beat of exciting soul-stirring music as the people danced and raised their hands toward the ceiling. Everyone joined in. It was as if they were cheering in adoration of something or someone special - and they were!

"The crowd listened, the crowd sang, and when the crowd cheered and got excited, their pounding feet on the stands thundered mightily through the quiet night announcing to the outside world that something very important was occurring in that round shaped metal building. And still the people came.

"Many years ago, there were tent people who came through town, talked about Jesus and sent people home healed 'through the power of God'. Under this big 'metal' tent, the believers gathered, sang, listened and went home healed 'through the power of God'. No rumors! No doubt! They walked where they had ridden, they ran where they had previously walked, they heard and talked where they were previously dumb, they saw things that were only objects and smells to them just hours before.

"Walking into the building no one could deny that

there was something special about this particular gathering of people. They were full of joy (and hadn't been drinking alcohol), they were happy (and not telling off-color jokes), they were friendly (and never asked for anything), they gave of themselves openly and freely (almost like they received more by giving rather than by receiving).

"Something definitely happened to me that night. I walked in feeling disgusted, disappointed with everything, my back hurting and feeling very lonely. Within minutes I was happy, I was hopeful, I was loved. Walking into the night, the lights I saw were not the gaudy carnival lights, but the glorious light that glowed around every individual that exited that building. I reached out my hand and saw that I glowed also. I turned to ask, 'What happened to me?' and instead of English, I was speaking another language.

"Someone nearby was laughing with utter abandon as they saw my amazement, 'That's the Holy Ghost speaking through you just like Charles taught from the stage!'

"As I continued walking away, joy overtook me also. I remembered something my grandmother used to read to me from the Bible, '...and everything you touch shall prosper.' Now, I understood. Everywhere I looked around the 'horse' barn on this special Friday evening, people were touching other people - hugging, praying for, laying hands on in Jesus' name. Bodies straightened up, people walked, grouchy people suddenly were laughing, sad people were crying with happiness. The one thing in common throughout was what everyone said, 'In Jesus' name!' and everything they touched 'prospered'.

"The lady on the stage, Frances Hunter, called for all the pregnant ladies or those who wanted to get pregnant to come to the front so she could lay hands on them. The next nine months will be particularly interesting to watch throughout central Florida. Frances laid hands on every pregnant lady in sight for a supernaturally fast delivery. Then she laid hands on all the barren women who came forward. The obstetricians better get geared up in the next few months because there is going to be a baby boom in Florida - in Jesus' Name!

"Grandma's favorite hymn was 'Onward Christian Soldiers' and I remember Grandpa whistling it as he drove around town. We sang it in church, too, but I never paid much attention to the words before. But, you know, as those anointed healing teams stepped forth and marched onto that floor, the noise, the thunder of their feet on the bleachers made them sound ten thousand strong, truly an army of God's soldiers marching onward to do battle and defeat the enemy.

"I must speak only for myself, but after being at what they called the 'Tampa Healing Explosion', I'm volunteering to join that army!

"What power! What love! What healings took place...all through ordinary people, some I've known for years!

"Praise God! I'm in His army now."

Let's go on the floor with the healing teams, shall we?

"What is your need?"

"Are you talking to me?"

"Yes!" the healing team member replied, chomping at the bit to see God work.

"Oh, I have a constant dull ache all around my back. I came today to get rid of the pain."

"O.K." she chirped excitedly. "That's easy! Sit over

here and we will grow out your legs."

"Well, I don't think so," he said, "You see, I have pain here in my hip, not in my legs."

Remembering our words to be *patient but persistent*, the healing team member assured the forty-five-year-old gentleman that "God doesn't sweat it. He can take care of a hip problem." Satisfied that they knew what they were doing, the man gingerly eased himself onto a chair. Placing both thumbs on the ankle bones, the "ordinary, turned-on" believer who had been trained to "lay hands on the sick" found that one leg was a whopping two inches shorter than the other. Then the command was given that the legs grow out, and all bones, ligaments, muscles, tendons, cartilage, vertebrae and discs be healed in the name of Jesus.

There was silence for a few moments until the other team member asked the man if he would like to take off his shoes. As he stood, his feet were flat on the floor with both legs of equal length. "Thank you, Jesus!" His hips were perfectly aligned and all pain was gone.

Later the man confessed, "I forgot to tell them that I was born with this condition, and I have worn built-up shoes all my life."

Let's go up on the stage where we can hear some of the miracles that just happened! These testimonies were given over the microphone for the audience to hear.

WOW! Did you hear about the young man who had a deaf ear for eighteen years? He said, "You know, the right ear drum was punctured right through when I was a boy of twelve. Really," he continued, "the healing team member didn't seem to understand what I said because she put her hands on my neck and moved my head around. All of a sudden I felt funny all over. I could hear my wife who was standing behind me crying. When I turned around she realized I could hear her and then she really cried - for joy! "

A beautiful young woman came forward to testify that "Today is my day! It's hard to believe that I came into this auditorium with excruciating pain in my left shoulder. For four months, the only relief I've had was in the form of steroid shots the doctor gave me in the shoulder area. A foreign speaking healing team member put her hands on me, and although I couldn't understand a word she said, except for 'In Jesus' name', all the pain left my body. Then I suddenly realized that the skin cancer on my face was gone. All the examiner could find was a slight scar-like mark on my cheek."

Another young woman said, "I was in an accident in 1984. It seemed everything inside me went from bad to worse from then until today. I came in with shooting pains in the bladder, the rectum and the female organs. The doctors had repeatedly scheduled me for surgery, but for some reason I did not consent to go into the hospital.

"Tonight I came knowing something would happen. I went over to the healing team members and both of them seemed to work on me at one time. One cast out the spirit of inheritance in Jesus' name while the other commanded a creative miracle in the affected area of my body in the name of Jesus.

"Something happened to me. I looked up from the floor to realize that I wouldn't need the pain relieving pills any more. All the pain was gone! "

Picture yourself in this situation.

"What can be done for a diagnosed case of Bell's Palsy? The eye closes, the face twitches and the bones of the face seem to be lopsided."

"Where is there help for me?"

"When I smile, my eye closes and won't stay open."

"When will something be done to help keep my eye open?"

"Who can help my face that is so distorted?"

All these questions went through the mind of a twenty-nine-year-old young man as he stood waiting for healing.

Suddenly, it was his turn and he was asked, "What's your problem?"

He quickly answered, "Bell's Palsy!" Later he related, "As soon as the words dropped from my lips, I realized the young men did not understand the magnitude of the disease, but they immediately got excited and said, 'No sweat for God!' They did something they called 'TNT'. My face began to tingle and move and it's all O.K. now!!"

Here's a good one!

A man had nerve deafness in the right ear for almost 20 years. The tests showed there was an 80% loss, and that it was deteriorating. The gentleman, about 62 years old, was so excited. As he listened, the sounds became clearer and clearer. While the healing team member did 'The Neck Thing', she lost him under the power of God. They left him on the floor and worked on someone else. After a period of time, he got up and found he could even hear the slightest whispers around him. The man was, as he put it, "Flabbergasted!!"

A very stoic teenager reported matter-of-factly that he had an accident trying to avoid an accident. "While riding my bike, a car swerved toward me. To avoid an impact, I turned, fell and slid under the very same car. Since that time, which was about two weeks ago, I have been living in heavy pain. My back was killing me and it was

impossible to sit any length of time. I couldn't do anything in school - gym, sports activities - nothing!

"Tonight I came with pain, and when the healing
team sat me down to grow out my legs, I could hardly
stand the pain until my legs actually grew out. To be
without pain was such a shock it took me a while to
realize it was gone. The freedom was great, to be able to
bend in half to the floor again! There was a memory of
pain only, as if a confirmation that the pain had been
there and was now gone! Thank You, Lord Jesus!"

A thirty-eight year old man with a ten-year history
of ulcerative colitis came to the Healing Explosion desperately looking for help. He had developed fistulas over
the past two years with much pain, bleeding and mucus.
A French speaking healing team member ministered to
him and the pain left immediately. Despite the fact that
they couldn't understand each other, God answered by
healing the man. Going immediately to check the discharge, he found the bleeding had stopped and the area
was drying up.

A lovely lady about thirty-eight years of age came to
report a lump about the size of a quarter or half dollar
under her right arm. Since the healing team consisted of
men, the woman put her hand on the lump and the men
put their hands on her arm. They commanded the lump
to go in Jesus' name, and then grew out her arms. As the
arm grew out, a tingling sensation went down the arm.
When she examined her armpit, the lump was gone.
Praise God!

"At fifty-eight years of age, I felt too young to be
bound by diabetes, heart trouble and two small strokes
that left my body with restricted movement and a lead-
weight feeling on the left side. I really had nothing to lose
as I walked into the Tampa Healing Explosion, expect-

ing God to meet me there. I wasn't disappointed, because when the command was given by a young healing team member, the spirit of death came out and the pressure on the one side of my head disappeared. Then she commanded a new pancreas and a new heart into me in Jesus' name. God really hears His children! When 'the neck thing' was laid on me in Jesus' name, my arm, neck, back and leg lost the heavy feeling and I had total freedom of motion! Now I know just how good our God really is!"

How can we ever hope to get all the "goodies" into one book? It is an impossibility, but we're trying to show you what happens in all areas, including finances. Here's an exciting report back from Tampa.

"My husband and I just attended your healing training and were on the Healing Team in Tampa on November 14th.

"During the training you had several offerings, of which in two of them we were especially moved by the Lord to give $1,000.00. The second offering that we were moved was Friday morning, you had a seed offering for ministries. Pastor Blonn told about giving for his ministry in an offering like this and how God honored it.

"My ministry started this past February as Director of the Pregnancy Center. We opened our doors July 1st and since then we have ministered to 107 women. We have been praying for a home for these girls. My husband gave me $10.00 for the offering and said he was going to the restroom. We didn't have any money in our account, but we had some in another account. I felt that strong urging from the Lord to give $1,000.00 and He would honor it. I wrote at the bottom of the envelope, 'I owe you $1,000.00.' I thought, 'Now, Lord, if this is really from You, my husband won't get upset when I show him what

I wrote.'

"He came back before the envelopes were collected and I showed it to him. At first he looked a little concerned, then just started singing and praising the Lord with a smile on his face and I knew it was okay. Praise the Lord! Oh, yes, and you said that this offering would be honored before Thanksgiving.

"This past Friday, November 21st, exactly one week after the offering, a woman from a certain foundation to whom I had sent information on the need of a home for girls in crisis pregnancy called. We have been working on this since March.

"She called and gave our ministry a beautiful home, cost $125,000. It has sixteen rooms, fully furnished, it has a little three room cottage over the workshop in the back. Praise the Lord! We will be able to house twenty girls in that home. Thank You, Jesus! We are so excited!"

And then of course, we love this one:

"Just wanted to share with you. Because of your meeting in 1985 in Tampa, and asking all 'singles' to stand and believe that your mate will come into your life by Christmas, enclosed is the result." (An invitation to the wedding accompanied the letter!)

This one thrilled us because it shows a continuation of what God wants for today!

"God's richest blessings on you both. I want you to know that your book and video *'How to Heal the Sick'* is marching on. We were privileged to be a part of showing these in three different church groups. Naturally or should I say supernaturally everyone has been touched - a change not only physically but mentally and spiritually to as many as will 'allow' God to move.

"The latest was a seventy-year-old lady who was injured at birth when the midwife pulled her tiny infant arm too hard at delivery. She has carried it across the front of herself because the arm would not bend. As a child she had to go through terrible exercises and casts with unbelievable pain. (You can imagine the medical knowledge and equipment and therapy of seventy years ago.)

"Anyway we showed a one hour segment of *"How to Heal the Sick"* video - then demonstrated the growing out of arms and legs. We wanted people to get involved. All doubt and unbelief left as adults and children saw and felt their own and others' limbs grow.

"The last one to come up was the pastor's mother (with the deformed arm). We laid hands on her and commanded the spine, muscles, etc. to be adjusted because she had back problems. Her legs were mentioned because she walked with a cane and then she told me she had disc problems and we ministered to that area plus neck and shoulder area for another problem as well as her arms. Because of the arm being as it was, we knew it was a different length. I laid hands on her again and asked the Lord to give her an 'overhaul'. She went out under the power which we found out afterward she didn't believe in - now she does.

"She remained there for quite awhile and her son laid hands on the arm and commanded it to be healed in Jesus' name. Pretty soon she began to move BOTH arms up in the air to a praise position while lying down.

"Everyone went wild! She was so drunk in the Spirit she couldn't get up. When she did get up much later, she was overwhelmed with the presence of God. She just kept moving her arms up and down as she returned to her seat. She took one son with one arm around his neck and her newly healed arm around her husband's neck and said, 'Now I can hug you!' She'd never been able to do that before. She was not even able to dress herself without help all these years!

"Nothing else was done while all this was going on - no other one was being ministered to. The Lord had the whole place in a joyous 'unglued' state. We instructed her to continue to speak to that arm and tell it to stretch and grow and strengthen.

"The next Sunday we wanted to check and see what all the Lord had done. We checked the arms and the legs and all were perfect. Arms are now the same length, no more back problems, discs are healed and she doesn't use or need the cane! She's one healed and turned-on Grandma! It's beautiful! Glory!"

"If Charles and Frances can do it, YOU can do it, too!"

Chapter Ten

KEEP EXPLODING!

by Frances

From the moment we walked into the Hyatt Regency Hotel, we knew that Kansas City was going to be something special. We had arrived a day early and found an air of excitement present even though none of the healing teams had arrived yet.

Wednesday morning began with an exciting program on KMBZ, the largest secular radio station in Kansas City. The interview was so exciting that T.V. Channels 4, 5 and 9 called for permission to interview us the night of the Healing Explosion.

When we returned to the hotel, representatives from both Channel 5 T.V. and the Kansas City Times were waiting for special interviews. God is moving on the secular media.

Later in the afternoon we came back to the hotel from yet another interview on a Christian radio station to find the hotel teeming with excitement as healing teams from all parts of the country brought an anticipation that was greater than anything we'd ever experienced!

The first night literally exploded as many of the healing teams were healed during the training sessions. The second day was equally thrilling as excitement continued to mount, especially when a busload of Navajo Indians unloaded at the hotel. Adding to the international flavor, John Howard and his wife Jacqueline arrived from Holland.

Thursday night was selected as the night to anoint pastors who wanted a fresh anointing and to operate in the Gifts of the Spirit more than they ever had before. Approximately 175 pastors had hands laid on them and went under the power of the Holy Spirit - never to be the same again!

I told a funny story from my book IF YOU REALLY LOVE ME. When I was in grammar school, a teacher asked who had parents who were born overseas. Some kids raised their hands. Then the teacher said, "Who had grandparents who were born overseas?" and many more raised their hands. Then "great-grandparents" and almost everyone raised their hands, all except me.

I will never forget the consuming lie I told when I was a little girl. I was always so much bigger than anyone else in my class. I wanted to cut off about six inches of my legs because I towered over all the boys. The other girls were petite, graceful and charming, and I pictured myself as a big cow who fell all over the place.

Praise God, I don't worry about things like that any more. Since I got saved, I discovered I'm a beautiful person because I've been created in the image of God. I'm smart, too, because I have the mind of Christ! That's the picture God painted on my mind when I was saved! It says so in His Word!

My people were all poor farmers who came from the river bottoms in Illinois. As the teacher came around the school room asking the other kids what country their relatives came from, I sat there like a little ugly duckling, and finally raised my hand.

"Yes, Frances," the teacher said.

With a poker face I said, "My grandfather is an Indian!"

In my little heart I thought about the best thing to be was a real Indian!

I told this story at the Kansas City training sessions, and then called the team of Navajo Indians forward. Some forty to forty-five Indians came forward, most of whom were saved and baptized with the Holy Spirit. What a standing ovation they received! They had come for additional training and to participate in a Healing Explosion so they could take the message back to the Navajo Indian Reservation! We laid hands on them for a special anointing. It was a special moment for all of us.

The Navajo Indians returned to their reservation and held their own special *Indian Healing Explosion* the next week at Shiprock, N.M. They really got the message!

During the Victory Breakfast on Saturday morning, the power of God was so strong that hardly anyone could stand up. The pastor of the First United Methodist Church in Shiprock, N.M. announced that one of the women in his congregation had listened to Charles as he ministered the baptism with the Holy Spirit the night before, but could not understand because she does not speak English. But, in the Navajo language she heard God say, "Be saved thoroughly!" God had communicated with this woman through Charles as he spoke in tongues in a language which Charles neither knows nor understands! This in itself is a miracle of God! ...Acts Chapter 2, 1987!

The excitement was tremendous at the Healing Explosion as approximately eight thousand people gathered at the Kemper Arena. The anointed praise and worship seemed to lift the entire audience, saved and unsaved, into the very heavenlies. Karen Wheaton's anointed singing was the "frosting on the cake" and she received a standing ovation for her rendition of "Satan, You're A Liar!"

The call for salvation and the baptism with the Holy Spirit brought some three thousand people streaming down the aisles. They looked like rivers of living water as they literally "flowed" onto the floor wanting the power of God in their lives. Many small children were standing on the front row, and they all received and spoke with "new tongues".

After receiving the baptism with the Holy Spirit and speaking in tongues for the first time, one of the new "babies" came up on the stage and ministered healing to a woman who was obviously in excruciating pain. An accident had knocked her spine out of line and injured her tailbone in addition to causing other damage.

This new baby spoke the commands, touched her "patient", and the woman was completely healed! The television crewmen got so excited, they looked like they were going to leap off the stage!

Even though we will only mention a few of the healing miracles, hundreds of healings occurred that exciting night in Kansas City at the Kemper Arena.

For example, many people came out of wheelchairs, including a boy from out of state who had been hurt in a mowing machine accident and was unable to walk. When the healing teams laid hands on him, the power of God restored him, and he walked.

A girl came up on the stage and reported that she had been unable to conceive, but I had laid hands on her two months before and now she was pregnant. This exciting testimony brought a steady stream of couples up to the stage for me to pray for them to have babies.

A woman who had not been able to hear out of one ear since she was seventeen months old reported she was hearing perfectly.

Miracles flowed constantly from the time the teams started ministering and never stopped until around midnight when the lights went out! The healing teams of Kansas City will never be the same - and neither will those who were ministered to on May 1, 1987!

The miracles continue...

"During the second training session, I was given a vision concerning the Explosion, but the Lord said it could be shared with you at a later time. The vision was that Kemper Arena was as a volcano during the service, as a mountain growing, rising until erupting. The eruption being the gold and silver (lava) streams spilling out and over and running down the sides and running out into the areas of cities, towns and rural areas around the Kansas City area.

"These gold and silver rivulets, in essence, represented each person who was there at Kemper Arena and they took a ribbon or rivulet of the gold and silver overflow back home with them. Then it spread from each one of those persons like threads, outward again, as they told of what they had seen, heard, learned or experienced from God and His Holy Spirit in that tremendous event.

"Also, during the service at Kemper, at the time of the mighty rush of the people down for the baptism with the Holy Spirit, there seemed to be a white vapor cloud gently whirling above the floor during the ministering of the Spirit.

"During the praise and worship in song, we were singing a song, 'God's Got an Army Marching Through the Land'. Everyone was clapping. I closed my eyes for a few minutes and the sound of the unison clapping hands brought forth the vision and the sound of thousands of marching feet, in unison and rank of the thousands of people in God's army that is beginning to march now, with His power and might. The sound seemed to grow so loud it was almost deafening for a few minutes. I really sense within that the Explosions that you are taking out to all areas of our country and the world are a very great part that is opening the gates into the world that have held God's army back for so great a number of years."

Truly, the army that is being raised up today is the end-time army of the believers and they are going forth around the world in great power, might, and zeal. Never in all of our lives have we ever seen people so turned on as they become at a Healing Explosion, and it doesn't go away!! They continue on with signs and wonders following!

Chapter Eleven

IF YOUR HEART IS STRONG, COME ALONG

by Frances

What an experience to see yourself on immense, mammoth billboards! Thirty of these "giants" announced the Healing Explosion in the city of Belem, Brazil. More than 10,000 posters and fliers were nailed to telephone poles, walls and wherever they found a place all over the city. We saw ourselves coming and going.

The day we arrived, a downpour of rain had completely saturated the field of the open air stadium where the meeting was to be held. We were very concerned about the mud; however God simply blew His breath and the field was totally dry before the meeting began.

A tremendous air of expectancy surrounded all of us the night of the first Healing Explosion ever held in Brazil (July, 1987).

Bob Barker shared with us that there was a rainbow over the moon just before we arrived at the stadium. All who had seen it exclaimed, "It is a sign from God!"

Because South Americans are notorious for not being on time, we were encouraged to arrive late. We were so excited we could hardly wait. When we arrived (on time) we discovered the stadium which holds 35,000 was already filled to capacity! The doors had been locked keeping thousands of people on the outside. We panicked! We agreed that we did not come to Belem to lock people out. We insisted that the doors be opened and the crowd allowed to stand on the field of the stadium.

What a sight! Thousands of human beings were standing on the great field, packed in as close as possible next to one another.

Even with twenty-five Green Beret Police and trained counselors making a human chain across the front of the platform, the pressing crowd was so great that nobody could keep them back. They were hungry for what God had for them!

There was an estimated crowd of over 60,000 at that first great Brazilian Healing Explosion, and yet many more were turned away because there was no room.

After worship and praise I read from a Portuguese Bible. A message reached us later that the people thought it was wonderful that I read the Bible in their language even though my accent was "terrible".

After a brief teaching on the miracle-working power of God and how God wanted to heal them, we ministered salvation to the entire audience and called for the baptism with the Holy Spirit. There was no way the people could come out of the stadium seats onto the field because the great soccer field was packed, but an estimated eighty percent of the people raised their hands to receive the baptism with the Holy Spirit.

While we were ministering the baptism, thousands of people began to pray in tongues. When close to sixty thousand people loudly and powerfully prayed in the Spirit at one time, God's glory came down. God took over the service as His power literally exploded with a thunderous crack!

The power of God in that stadium was something

none of us had ever experienced before. It was actually almost frightening because it was so strong!

They continued to pray. They were excited about their new tongues. You could actually feel the power building more and more!

I looked at Charles and said, "Honey, we just lost the service!" I knew in my spirit that was exactly what happened so I looked at Charles while these sixty thousand people were praying loudly and fervently in tongues and said, "Let's join them!"

We continued praying in the Spirit and we could feel the power of God increasing and increasing and faith was igniting. After possibly fifteen minutes of praying in tongues (they don't stop like we do in America), I held up my hand for them to stop, and they thought I was waving at them, so they waved right back at me and continued praying in tongues, only they increased the volume.

I looked up at God and said, "God, what are we going to do now?"

We didn't have to do one thing! God did it all!

Suddenly, an empty wheelchair went up in the air and was passed up to the stage, then came another empty wheelchair - then came another wheelchair - then came a stretcher with no one on it - then came crutches - then came another wheelchair.

Then somebody screamed, "She was blind and now she can see!" They brought two children to the stage who had been deaf and their ears were now totally healed!

A scream rose from the audience at the end of the field. Our interpreter said the people were yelling, "Look at the orange shirt!" We had no idea what that meant but we looked until we finally located a man with an orange shirt running around the outside perimeter of the field, with about a hundred people following him. The number swelled to about five hundred people trying to catch him.

After running nearly a quarter of a mile around the track, he ran up to the stage, hugged both of us and exclaimed, "I'm not even a Christian, and God healed me!" Then he added, "Please, I want to be a Christian!" We took care of that real fast! Then through our interpreter we heard his story!

He had been in an automobile wreck about four years before which had severed his spine causing paralysis from his waist down. As he sat on the field, he began to feel life in his legs again and realized he could walk. Not only did he walk! HE RAN!

God had to do a second great miracle to restore the atrophied muscles, lungs, and strength to run nearly a quarter mile.

He went running and leaping, and praising God! "So he, leaping up, stood and walked and entered the temple with them - walking, leaping, and praising God" (Acts 3:8).

God is re-enacting the book of Acts through His disciples of this end-generation harvest of souls!

We never regained control of the service again because God's power just kept moving supernaturally through the people. Crippled bodies were made straight and children were healed!

One little girl managed to make her way up to the edge of the stage. Through an interpreter, I said to the pastor of the Assembly of God church, "You lay hands on her." He laid hands on this little child who had also been injured in an automobile accident and she was totally and completely healed by the power of God. Her damaged little legs instantly straightened out!

The tears that were shed were just incredible. All of us who had come from the United States could do nothing but stand there and weep at the presence and the power of God.

We repeated over and over, "God wants to heal you. God wants to heal you. God's a miracle working God." God's power just exploded in demon possessed and oppressed people and they were set free! While we will never know the end result of this until we get to heaven, those of us who were there know we all experienced something that we had never experienced in our lives before.

The pressing crowd surged forward into the stage area in spite of the security we had, and an entire cordon of police was necessary to assist us in getting through the people to the exits.

The thing that thrilled us the most was the fact that after we left, the crowd began to thin down allowing the healing teams room to minister to the people. A little boy whose body was totally crippled from cerebral palsy was healed by the power of God as a healing team member laid hands on him.

A skull which was not closed, closed instantly when another team member ministered. It didn't just start to close, but the entire skull closed completely!

The mother had been told that her child was going to be mentally retarded. However she felt confident that the supernatural power of God had totally healed the child.

There were many other healings which took place through the trained Brazilian healing team members after we had left the stadium. The excitement and miracles spurred them on to continue laying hands on the sick. Back at the hotel after the meeting, we enjoyed a great time of celebration for all God had done for the Brazilian people.

A. L. Gill said, "I do not believe that anything like this has ever happened in the history of the world! "

An Assembly of God pastor wept like a baby and finally left the stage during the meeting and just stood there and cried and cried. He kept sending me a message saying, "I have never seen anything like this in all my life".

NONE OF US HAD EITHER!

During our time of sharing at the hotel, we asked what others felt was the most exciting or outstanding thing they felt during the meeting.

One of the men on our team said, "It was the look on the peoples' faces as they all stood there. The hunger in their eyes as they looked at whoever was speaking on the stage was absolutely incredible because every eye in that entire stadium was full of hope."

As I had left to go to the stadium earlier in the evening, I said, "God, I don't really feel very anointed tonight. I hope You are! "

He certainly was because He really demonstrated His mighty power and glory like we have never seen nor will we ever forget, nor will any of us ever be the same again. To God be the glory!

The local church presented me with a beautiful bouquet of red roses. As the wife of the Assembly of God pastor gave them to me, she said, "These roses will wither and fade away and their fragrance will disappear, but the fragrance that you brought to Belem will last until eternity." (I did my share of crying at that point.)

The next day when we arrived at the Goiania airport, four people were standing on the airfield with signs that said, "Charles and Frances Hunter, we love you. Welcome! " As we walked into the airport, a choir of over one hundred people greeted us with the most glorious songs that you ever heard. All of us wept because of the love of these people and their desire to find more of God.

We ministered in two Assembly of God churches on Sunday night, where the enthusiasm was tremendously high. Both had warned us that we would not see nearly the crowd on a Monday night that we had seen on a Saturday night in Belem.

Again we were surprised when we arrived at the open air stadium to find a crowd even greater than that in Belem. The stadium was larger and the open field was larger.

For reasons we do not understand, the stadium officials have a tendency to lock the doors in the stadium once the seats are filled. After much discussion, they finally opened the gates and allowed probably another fifteen thousand people in. With the stadium seats and field filled to capacity, they again locked the doors and turned away several thousand more people.

When it was time for us to speak to the estimated crowd of over 60,000, again we felt a tremendous hunger for the power of God.

Hoping to make a call for the baptism with the Holy Spirit and have the people come to the field, we had temporarily stationed the healing teams arm-in-arm several layers deep approximately two hundred feet from the platform.

Once we saw the thousands of hungry people, we realized we could not bring people down out of the stands and through the mob that was standing on the actual stadium field.

To prevent a stampede, we asked the healing teams to begin walking forward very slowly toward the stage. Then we told them the power of God would be with them as they walked. Some of the healing team members who were in the crowd said the people got up out of their wheelchairs and walked "with" the crowd as the Spirit of God fell upon them.

Again the night was beautiful. This time God had supernaturally sent doves to fly over the stadium as a sign from God that His Holy Spirit was present. It was beautiful to look up and to see the doves circling over the stadium.

The next thing we saw was the stadium field totally filled with the presence of angels. At the same time, we saw the glory cloud of God descend over the area. So we knew once again that God was going to do some tremendously supernatural things.

After a few minutes of teaching, we ministered the baptism with the Holy Spirit. Again, the response seemed to be about 80% as hands were raised all through the crowd indicating they desired all God wanted to give them.

It was another great night to remember! In the United States it often seems like people have sort of a "ho-hum" attitude during the ministering of the baptism with the Holy Spirit. "Well if I get it, I get it; if I don't get it, I don't get it and I'm not real sure that I want it anyway".

Brazilian response was tremendous! When they received, there was an explosion of the power of God. They were like an empty sponge just waiting to soak up the power!

Many of our team members were stationed in strategic places around the field and in the stands. They all said the same thing, "Everybody around us began speaking in tongues at one time." When tens of thousands begin to speak in tongues at one time, there is power!

As this miraculous power spread through the crowd, once again people began passing crutches, canes, and various other devices up to the stage. We did not see as many wheelchairs passed up to the stage as we did in Belem. However, Charles felt that the percentage of healings was even higher than at Belem.

Since ministering to individuals was totally impossible, we had them lay their hands on their heart if they needed a new heart, their pancreas if they need a new pancreas, their ears for hearing, and many other different parts of the body. They were so full of simple faith, it was easy for them to be healed.

When we asked how many of them had actually felt the power of God in the part of their body that was sick and KNEW that they were healed, raised hands were seen all over the audience. God had not healed just one or two - thousands and thousands had felt His healing power.

The Brazilian people have a tremendous love and desire to touch you (and receive their healing). There were times when it was a little on the frightening side, especially when you have tens of thousands of people out there all reaching for you.

At one point in the service, we bound the devil in the name of Jesus and commanded the foul tormenting spirits to come out of the people.

Between 60,000 excited expectant people praying in tongues, our binding the devil and casting out demons, what happened next was inevitable.

At the name of Jesus those demons have to come out, and you never saw such a display of demonic activity in your life.

One demon-possessed woman started running toward the stage knocking everybody down that came within ten feet of her. She would pick big men up and throw them. Security quickly removed the platform steps to keep her from getting up on the eight foot high stage.

After having such an evidence of the power of God in Belem, and now in Goiania, I very confidently said, "In the name of Jesus, you foul tormenting devil, I command you to come out of her!"

That didn't stop that devil one single bit! I repeated it, only this time I was a little louder and a little more emphatic!

She kept right on coming, throwing people out of her way. I must have repeated "In the name of Jesus, you foul tormenting devil, I command you to come out of her" at least fifteen times, but she kept right on coming. She was getting super close to the stage, just as devil-tormented as she ever was. By this time, my heart was beating a little faster than normal, and I repeated the command a little louder and a little more emphatic. She kept right on coming!

I'm going to be real honest with you. At a time like this you can think of a lot of things in the twinkling of an eye, and probably the first thought the devil would have liked for me to believe was, "Is the name of Jesus really more powerful than the devil?" The second thought was, "Get behind Charles and let him protect you," but I knew once I gave up control of the situation, everything was lost, so I stood my ground, even when she was now about two feet from where I was standing eight feet above her on the stage.

I said, "In the name of Jesus, SHUT UP!"

Someone screamed at the side of the soccer field, and I looked up and away from this woman, and when I looked back, there was no longer a demon-possessed woman there. I wondered what had happened to her and didn't discover the real answer until about a month later when I was going through some pictures of Brazil. I saw a series of pictures showing an opening in the crowd where this woman was throwing people around. The final picture showed this same woman, completely clothed and in her right mind, standing there with the greatest look of love you could ever imagine! No wonder I didn't recognize her - the demons had finally given up and fled and she was covered with the peace of God. I looked again and again. It was the same dress, the same hairdo, the same everything except an insane woman was now made whole by the power of God and the name of Jesus!

Many deaf people, especially children, were healed. Parents literally "passed" their children through the crowd to the healing team members so they could be healed.

It was beautiful to see the faith of the Brazilian people, how they love God and believe Him for miracles.

But the most moving fact is when they want to touch you, they don't "see" you at all, they see Jesus living inside of you!

Reports from the local Christian leaders said the crowd was double the size of any other Christian meeting that had ever been held in the city of Goiania. They added that it was the first meeting they had ever seen that exhibited such great power.

The pastors in the local churches also invited us to come back again, promising they will fill the 100,000 seat stadium to the top with excited Brazilian people next time.

We excitedly went on to Sao Paulo in preparation for the Healing Explosion in Campinas. We were praying that God would do it again!

Sao Paulo, the second largest city in Brazil, has a population of approximately sixteen million people and teems with activity.

The first night we went to a Spirit-filled Baptist church. This took us into a totally different era or culture of Brazil because these people wore make-up and earrings and danced before the Lord during the praise and worship.

The Sunday prior to our visit there, the pastor's wife was reading to the congregation from the book *"HOW TO HEAL THE SICK"* and a crippled child's body was straightened out as it was healed!

Because of this, of course, there was great joy and anticipation of our visit there. The spirit of the meeting was absolutely incredible because you could just literally feel the power of God.

After we spoke a while, we had an extremely interesting word of knowledge. We said, "There is someone who has a pain in the kidney area, but it is just about an inch or two away from the spine. It's either someone who has been shot or someone who had a knife wound. Who is it?"

A man who had been shot eight years before immediately leaped to his feet. He had been in extreme pain ever since because of the bullet wound. The crowd was amazed at how we could have known this, and so were we, except God knows everything.

When we commanded the pain to come out and commanded all the scar tissue, the burned and destroyed muscles, nerves, ligaments, tendons and tissues to be restored in Jesus' name, the man was instantly healed!

Rejoicing took over the entire church when the man was totally healed! We had several other words of knowledge and we did our best to lay hands upon all the sick. Individual ministry was extremely difficult because every church we visited was packed wall to wall and the aisles totally filled. However, the teams ministered after we left and miracles, signs, and wonders followed every trained believer.

The next night we went to the largest Assembly of God church in Sao Paulo. It is one of the most ornate buildings in which we have ever ministered. Most of the building was done in marble and was decorated with gold leaf roses.

It had to be a church of young people because it was necessary to climb two flights of steep stairs to reach the sanctuary. When we finally reached the pulpit area, we looked up to discover two high balconies above us. And every corner of this most unique church was literally running over with people.

It is impossible for us in the United States to understand how they pack the people into the churches until you actually witness it.

Approximately seventy-five pastors from other churches were also there. This particular Assembly of God Church has "mothered" about 700 other churches which have a combined membership of approximately 150,000.

It is estimated that there are thirteen million members of the Assemblies of God in Brazil. Charles had prayed months before when eight million members had been reported. "God, let us train eight million members of one denomination in one nation how to heal the sick and how to minister the baptism with the Holy Spirit!"

Can you imagine eight, or thirteen million Spirit-filled believers who not only were filled with God's power, but knew how to dispense it, attacking a nation of 140,000,000 people?

We all know Jesus is coming back soon and we are seeing His church prepare for His arrival! Hallelujah!

Again the move of the Spirit in this church was absolutely incredible. While there was great excitement and great emotion during all the meetings, we discovered that many of them do not speak in tongues. In every church a tremendous number of people received the baptism with the Holy Spirit.

With such crowds jamming the seats, aisles, stairs and balconies, laying hands on the sick was going to be a problem. God spoke and said that we were to walk down through the crowd and lay hands on everybody we could touch.

The healing teams that were with us surrounded us so those we could not touch, they could. Just as we began, Charles climbed up on one of the pews. With all the people standing, he walked up and down the pews and laid hands on everybody. What a sight to see him crawling over pews!

It was a night of great power and glory as people were healed all over that church.

When we asked how many had been healed, at least 70% to 75% of the audience raised their hands indicating they had been healed.

Manoel Ferreira, president of the Assembly of God in Brazil, was the one who invited us to come to Brazil. He drove to Sao Paulo to be with us and there was great rejoicing as he saw what God did.

The pastors of the other churches were so excited and insisted that we come back to Sao Paulo to the 150,000 seat arena which they say would be filled every night if we would minister there for three nights.

There is a great spiritual hunger in Brazil. These people want a living Jesus. There is nothing blasé, there is nothing half-hearted about their hunger for teaching from the Word of God.

The next night we visited Manoel Ferreira's church in Campinas. Brother Ferreira not only pastors a church but he is president of one of the two branches of the Assemblies of God in Brazil.

Again the church was packed out wall to wall. They had a 20 x 20 foot television screen outside the church on the parking lot. The people not only filled the parking lot but they overflowed into the street watching the massive screen and what was happening inside the church. There were nearly as many people outside as there were inside the church that night. The hunger is so great and the churches are too small.

The praise and worship here is loud and exciting and the people really participate. We discovered you do not clap in some churches because they believe when you clap you bring in the devils. However, in Pastor Ferreira's church there was clapping and loud rejoicing as we praised and worshiped God.

It was another one of those tremendous nights when many, many people received the baptism with the Holy Spirit. While we called out a few to receive healing through the word of knowledge, most of the healing was done as once again we walked through the audience and over the tops of the pews. The healing teams from the United States were sent outside to minister to the masses.

The Brazilian people are so hungry to see a living Jesus that they believe if you'll just touch them they'll be healed. But then that's what the Word of God says, isn't it? "Those who believe shall lay hands on the sick and they shall recover."

The word had spread all over Brazil. When Pastor

Manoel met us in Sao Paulo he said, "I have traced you from the moment you arrived in Brazil. The pastors have said, 'You did not tell us to expect as much as we got.'"

Every pastor in every city had reported that they had received much more than they had anticipated from our meetings in their cities. Praise God, He always gives exceedingly, abundantly over what we ask or think.

When we arrived at our hotel in Campinas, we were met by newspaper reporters. They were not Christian and of course asked the usual questions, "How do you heal the sick? How do you know they're healed? How long does it take to heal someone?"

We said, "Do any of you have a back problem?"

The cameraman said, "Do I ever!" Through the Portuguese interpreter he explained, "I have a problem in my upper back and lower back. I am really hurting right now. Can God heal me?"

Of course, that was all we needed. We sat him down and grew out his legs as the two reporters watched in amazement. We stood him up and grew out his arms.

THE MAN WAS TOTALLY HEALED!

God is so good because He always grants us exciting miracles like that at just the right moment to make a great impact on the press! Imagine - the excellent newspaper article reported that the photographer was healed by the power of God as an instant witness to unbelievers and as a preview to all the miracles that were to come in Campinas.

The Healing Explosion in Campinas was the only Explosion that was held inside of an auditorium. As we entered the building, we looked at the thousands of people standing jammed together on a concrete floor. The whole scene reminded us of a can of Vienna sausages which are packed in super tight. Knowing that it would be three or four hours before they would have the opportunity to sit, they stood there with tremendous expectation on their faces.

The seats in the bleachers were filled including the dugouts designed for the press at the very top of the auditorium. Everywhere you looked, you saw a mass of faces.

The auditorium officials estimated between ten and twelve thousand were inside the building while thousands more stood outside watching on the big TV screens. As we walked down into the arena to minister to the very badly crippled people, we could only go a short ways because of the massive crowd packed one against another.

One rather aged blind man was pushed through the crowd until he stood in front of us. As we laid our hands on him, we commanded the spirit of blindness to come out and his eyes to open.

Suddenly he looked up, excitement obviously building on his face, waved his hands and yelled, "Gloria Deus! Gloria Deus! Gloria Deus! Gloria Jesus! Gloria Jesus!"

He was wildly excited because once he was blind but now he could see!

Because of the press of the crowd, it was impossible for an interpreter to be with us to explain every problem and/or situation as we ministered and laid hands on people. So when crippled legs straightened out and several people got out of their wheelchairs, we just praised God for it and went on expecting another miracle for the next person and the next and the next. The building was so jammed, those in wheelchairs who were healed couldn't walk far because there was no room! But the healings were so obvious that great joy filled the entire building!

There seems to be a tremendous amount of deafness in Brazil and God really blessed with the healing of deaf ears. One little girl had never heard a single solitary sound according to her mother. After she was healed, I tested her ears with very simple sounds because I didn't know enough Portuguese to test her in Portuguese. She repeated all the sounds because she understood perfectly.

Before we had gone into the crowd to minister, we explained what we were going to do through an interpreter. When we approached a person, we would say, "Silver and gold have we none, but such as we have, we give it to you, and in the name of Jesus Christ of Nazareth rise up and walk". And then we would motion for them to rise.

It's difficult to describe the expressions on people's faces when they suddenly realize they have been healed.

One rather aged man was sitting in a chair with his walking stick by his side. He must have thought, "They really mean that! They really mean that!" Suddenly, he rose up and was amazed that his feet held him up. He held his walking stick high in the air and rejoiced that he was no longer crippled!

On and on and on and on went the miracles. Since it was impossible to minister to the thousands of people, we prayed en masse for them and then we told them as clearly as we could, "Check your bodies!"

Since there was no way to determine the healings in such a large crowd, through the interpreter we told them, "If you know you're healed and your body is better, your body can move where it couldn't and the pain is gone, raise your hands and wave them at Jesus!" Well over half the crowd appeared to be waving their hands indicating that they had been healed.

Again the baptism with the Holy Spirit was absolutely phenomenal. It looked like possibly 80% of the people again raised their hands when we asked, "How many of you do not speak in tongues?"

They were excited to know they too could receive the dynamic power of God's Holy Spirit. When we ministered we couldn't stop them from speaking in tongues. It was so loud and so powerful that we believe even hundreds, maybe thousands of people were healed as they were speaking in tongues. We couldn't shut them up! They continued for more than ten minutes, very loudly.

Then we tried to get them singing in tongues. At first we were not successful. Apparently they don't sing in tongues in Brazil. With our persistence and Bob Barker singing over the microphone in tongues, they began to harmonize together and went from speaking in tongues into singing in tongues; like Paul said, "I pray with my understanding and I pray with my spirit. I sing with my understanding and I sing with my spirit." That is when the power of God really broke!

We believe well over 100,000 received the baptism with the Holy Spirit in this short series of Healing Explosions, and there is no way to measure the number who were saved and healed, but great multitudes were touched.

"And great multitudes followed Him..." (Matthew 4:25).

A part of our hearts was left in Brazil. When we returned home on Sunday, we were ready to go back on Monday.

You cannot stand in the glory and power of God and feel His mighty presence without something happening to you individually. We're going to do all we can

to satisfy the spiritual need of those beautiful, spiritually
hungry people!

Chapter Twelve

THE MIRACLES OF
THE WILD WEST

By Frances

We knew from the very start that Portland was going to be fabulous, because we had the largest number at our pastors' luncheon we had ever had. The excitement was tremendous, and we started 193 video healing schools to train healing teams for the Healing Explosion.

And what an explosion it was! We outgrew the ballroom at the hotel with healing teams and had to move our Friday meeting to the Coliseum where we anointed the healing teams after giving them "the charge"!

When the worship started, over a thousand people came down on the floor to praise Him in the dance, and everyone felt a tremendous anticipation from the audience.

Many people were healed of cancer as they came down on the floor at the beginning of the service. We had the greatest number with cancer we had ever seen!

The newspaper and TV coverage reported ten thousand people attended the meeting, and 4,500 received the baptism with the Holy Spirit. What a revival that brings! And just as it happened in Brazil, a man jumped out of his wheelchair without anyone laying hands on him. There was hardly room enough on the floor of the Coliseum to hold those who came for the baptism.

It was a night for the healing of scoliosis! Many people came to the stage and reported their backs straightened out and pain left as healing teams laid hands on them. Multiple sclerosis disappeared, and numerous people came out of wheelchairs. Many people were healed of deafness. There were so many healings we couldn't keep up with them! A girl born with club feet was healed and the two feet became the same size instantly!

It's happening in AMERICA!

Tune in to these testimonies which resulted from the Portland, Oregon Healing Explosion.

"My sister, who is Baptist, was one of your trained team members in Portland. The Sunday after the Explosion found the entire church talking about healing and had team members ministering in the service with a healing line.

"One of my customers, a mainline Baptist type organization, witnessed one of their people healed of a back problem. This person had been in bed for one year because of his injury. It has the whole facility in a tizzy.

"I have heard no denominational back stabbing or negative remarks from the evangelical association or members, either openly or quietly. In fact, I have heard several encouraging remarks about the thousands who came forward for the Holy Spirit.

"I personally was moved to tears more than once that Friday evening, recognizing that Portland would never be the same! Praise God!"

"Since you made us promise to write and relate some

of the exciting events that took place at the Explosion, I thought I'd hop to it.

"To say it was a life-changing event would be an understatement.

"When the two of you and Bob and Joan began to lay hands on us for the anointing, all three of us looked at each other and that huge Coliseum and wondered what were we doing there? Satan thought he would throw one last dart at us.

"When you (Frances) put your hand on my head and asked for the anointing to be imparted, it was like a bolt of lightning went right down through me and flooded me with peace and all my doubts were gone. It was almost as strong as the first time you laid hands on me to receive the baptism with the Holy Spirit back in the early 70's in Tacoma, Washington. With that event, God totally changed my life."

"You asked for reports and I do have one. The second day after I got home from the Portland Explosion a friend called to tell me about her sister, due for gall bladder surgery. Well, for the greater glory of the Lord, I drove to her house and did exactly as we were taught and made a new friend and went home.

"Three days later her sister called to say she would not need the surgery. The polyp blocking the duct was gone! She had not told me about the polyp - only that she had to have gall bladder surgery.

"So, as Charles did, I spoke into her a new one fresh from God's warehouse! "

"Enclosed is my check for $1,000 that takes care of an IOU that I made to God at the conference. The Lord has done numerous miracles financially and I am a firm

believer in investing in the kingdom as a demonstration
of my trust in God my Father. Though I committed to
make this offering in Portland, I had to wait until I returned from Hawaii to write the check. The neat thing
was that before I could get the check written, God had
cleared the way for an insurance settlement that will pay
me more than $16,000 this week, in spite of people saying
contrary. I have chosen to trust God and not walk in fear
or strife. I'm believing though for an even greater return
because of the season we are in. As the Word says, 'the
desires of the righteous will be granted.'"

"Another one of our members had invited his family
from Seattle to come to the Healing Explosion. His
mother, father, grandmother and two sisters came.
Saturday after the 'Explosion' they went out for lunch
at a restaurant near our home. As they were finishing
their meal, his grandmother had a stroke. They called us
and asked if they could bring her here for prayers. When
they came, the left side of her face was drooping, she had
no control of her tongue or mouth, and could not talk, she
had much fear and confusion. We bound Satan, cast out
the spirit of death and stroke and commanded, in the
name of Jesus, a sound mind and her body to return to
normal. Within twenty minutes she was back to normal.
Her face was back to normal, the color came back, she
was able to talk perfectly and all confusion and fear was
gone - no problems since. Thank you Lord!"

"During a 'prove-me' offering, Frances said that
someone would receive from the Lord on or before February 14, 1987. Our need seemed great and February was
our wedding anniversary. We remembered Frances'
words and as February 14th approached, we would en-

courage one another with the hope of receiving God's provision.

"We had gotten into a season of prayer beginning at 4 a.m. and on one February morning as we were ending prayer about 6 a.m. the doorbell rang. A friend was at the door. As my husband opened it, this friend handed him an envelope and said that the Lord had told her to come then and give it, hugged him, said she loved us and turned and left.

"When we opened the envelope there was $1500 cash and we were stunned - immediately the 'prove me' offering came to our minds and we thanked and praised God for His goodness and faithfulness. For us the timing and the amount were miracles.

"Other times we had heard dates given for people to receive blessings. This time as Frances spoke we got a hold of this date for us and by February 14th we had used the $1500 to meet the needs for which we had been asking God to provide!"

"These weeks following the Portland Healing Explosion have been a time for prayerful consideration of a truly 'mountain top' experience. It indeed has changed my life. I want to bring you up-to-date.

"My brother, who publishes the Northwest paper 'Christian Update' attended the Explosion. He told me this:

"Kathy (his wife) and I have attended many, many events but never have we felt so completely sure of the Spirit's presence in all that was said and done. We felt total peace that the Lord was having His own way at all times. We were at ease right from the beginning. He said that you have taught the will of God with the truth and pureness so often lost to greed. He was impressed by the 'ordinariness' of Charles and Frances Hunter...'servants of the Lord!'"

If you have any doubt about long distance prayer working, you won't have when you finish this next story:

During the Portland Healing Explosion in July, we learned of the abduction and brutal beating of a Seattle pastor's young daughter. She had been left unconscious in a drainage ditch with her head underwater. Initial reports claimed the child was brain dead.

Immediately all fourteen hundred of the healing team trainees joined us in binding the devil and speaking healing over the child.

During the Healing Explosion, a progress report reached the stage stating that she was still critical, but her little bruised and battered body was at least responding. We again prayed en masse for her total healing.

Does "long distance" prayer work? Oh, yes! Jesus' power is not limited by walls or distance. Read this article from a recent "local" newspaper regarding her "miraculous" recovery:

HOSPITAL DISCHARGES ELLENSBURG TODDLER

"Describing Theresa Johnson's recovery as 'miraculous' and 'unexpected', doctors at Seattle's Children's Orthopedic Hospital agreed to discharge the Ellensburg girl this afternoon.

"A discharge panel of eleven health professionals reviewed the toddler's case Thursday afternoon and 'decided she had recovered almost completely and is ready to go home,' according to Dean Forbes, a hospital spokesman.

"The child has been hospitalized since July 30 after she was abducted and beaten near her Ellensburg home.

"Theresa's speech is not yet fully recovered and she will need to continue seeing a speech therapist in Ellensburg. That, however, is the only therapy the young girl will need.

"Forbes said there is some concern the child's vocal chords were damaged during intubation. On two occasions a tube was inserted in Theresa's throat to help her breathe. Forbes said Theresa is scheduled to return to the hospital next week to have her throat checked."

In addition to the newspaper coverage, the local television station monitored the child's progress. The anchor man reported very plainly that many people had been praying for her complete recovery. Even the news media gave credit to the Lord.

Praise God! Prayer works!

Another miracle!

"Hallelujah for the Portland Healing Explosion! The two-and-a-half days of training plus the Friday night at the Coliseum were the greatest in my life. And I've been around a long time. My profession is that of a registered nurse and at sixty-six years of age I am now realizing the full impact of God's purpose for me in the healing ministry.

"The reality of God also lies in another area. Of the several collections that were taken throughout the week there were two that are remarkably impressed in my spirit and mind. For the 'prove me collection' I was going to put in a big $20.00 but the Lord had me add another zero and make it $200.00.

"Then for the collection to receive the greatest desire

of our hearts, I was prepared to put a big $10.00 in for a friend's healing. But the Lord had me add another zero and make it $100.00. By Friday noon I took a peek at my checkbook balance and there wasn't enough to pay the hotel bill via check so I had to charge that, a total contradiction of my financial conscience. However, I was at such remarkable peace, a peace beyond explaining or understanding, that I fretted not. I bet you can guess why.

"When I arrived home about 1 a.m. there were two calls on my recorder. A clerk in the Bankruptcy Court in Chicago had left a message she had a check for me and needed my address verified. The check was for over $22,000 (yes, twenty-two thousand dollars) paying me for payrolls I had to pay that were not my responsibility. As a creditor in a large bankruptcy case of several years ago I had thrown all my records away on the basis of total futility. But some clever lawyers in the bankruptcy court petitioned the judge to subrogate my claim in front of the IRS and Small Business Administration. The judge agreed and set a legal precedent! The justice of our God reigns."

Chapter Thirteen

BETTER THAN BAR-B-QUED RIBS

By Charles and Frances

Let's go from the west coast to the central part of the nation, shall we? Don't miss a single Healing Explosion, because each one of them has its own unique and different flavor as you've already seen.

The Cleveland Healing Explosion started off with a bang. As soon as we arrived, we had to dash to a radio station for an exciting interview program. From there we rushed back to a press conference at the hotel.

During our entire stay, we were competing with the Annual National Rib Burn-Out in downtown Cleveland, Ohio, next to the Convention Center. All of the famous barbecue cooks around the world presented their unique blend of barbecue sauces. All types of barbecued foods were sold on the already jammed streets making transportation difficult, but that didn't stop God and His miracles at the Cleveland Convention Center on August 14, 1987.

The first night of our training sessions we ministered to a fireman who had a back problem caused by a falling building ten years previously and he had suffered much pain ever since. We did "the neck thing", "the leg thing", "the arm thing" and "the pelvic thing" - in other words we did "the total thing". He was totally and completely healed.

We had the opportunity to share this miracle on the "A.M. Cleveland" NBC television talk show bright and early on Thursday morning. The gracious host allowed us approximately twelve minutes to tell the Cleveland audience all about the Healing Explosion.

Every Friday from 12 noon to 1 p.m., a "Prayer on the Square" is sponsored by Pastor Ward Potts of the Christ the King Lutheran Church. He had invited us to be guest speakers and little did we realize this was going to happen in the middle of Cleveland during a Friday noon hour.

Dismissing all the healing teams at noon, we all walked to the Square. Can you imagine what downtown Cleveland thought as they heard us all shout "Jesus" five times in a row at the top of our lungs? There is power in the name of Jesus and it literally resounded for blocks around. Some members of our staff were on the fourteenth floor of the hotel with the windows shut and they could hear everything we said because the acoustics were so fantastic.

Then we asked the healing teams to turn first to the north, then south, then east and then west and we commanded Satan to let our people go and allow them in to the Healing Explosion on Friday night. What an exciting thing to see 1,400 people standing on a public square at the noon rush hour lifting up Jesus!

The city of Cleveland proclaimed August 14, 1987 as the official "Hunter Healing Explosion Day" and we were presented a beautiful proclamation signed by the mayor of the city.

We were delighted when the councilman, (a born-again Christian), presented it to us. He announced the proclamation over the loud speakers and what a joy it was to see him fly the banner of Jesus. He also told the audience that the mayor of Cleveland is a born-again Christian. What a blessing to be in a city where God has touched the lives of some of the top officials!

The excitement as we walked into the Convention Center on Friday night was just unexplainable. We saw and felt the presence and the power of God.

Faith was exploding as the people came to receive from God. One man was being dragged in as he hung on to the shoulders of two friends. He was obviously dying of cancer.

When we made the call for people with cancer to come forward, approximately two hundred people lined up to be healed. What an opportunity for God to show His power!

Charles saw the man we had watched being dragged in by his friends. He immediately ran over to this man, laid hands on him and said, "Silver and gold have I none, but such as I have I give unto thee. In the name of Jesus Christ of Nazareth, rise up and walk, and RUN!"

The man got up, grabbed Charles' hand and began to run as fast as the two of them could run, down the center of the Convention Center and all the way back. The screaming crowd stood to their feet and praised God for His healing power.

Cleveland is over for our part. However, the work for the healing teams has just begun. They are going throughout the area operating in power and making "Supernatural House Calls" ministering to the people in their homes, on the streets, in the grocery stores.

A friend wrote about "wavering faith" and it will help you!

"I just returned from the Cleveland Explosion, and I just have to write this letter. The Lord has been speaking to me all of this year. He told me to go to Cleveland, and, on blind faith, I went. I love the Lord with all my heart, and I have given my life to Him but there have been doubts as to whether He would heal through me. My faith wavered.

"When I got to Cleveland, I realized I had forgotten my checkbook. At the first two offerings I put in $10.00 each time. During the sessions I could see all the deep, strong faith you have for the Lord and the confidence you have in His healing power through you. I was feeling so empty inside, and I knew it was because of my wavering faith and the fact that I should have been putting more in the offering. I made up my mind to put $50.00 in the Thursday afternoon offering. I felt pretty good. However, when the time came to listen to God's voice, He said to put in $100.00, and I did. I thought to myself, 'I can't believe I'm doing this.' My spirit began to lift as the afternoon and evening sessions went on. I knew the Lord had tested my obedience. At each session I put in what He told me. I can never thank you enough for all the lessons you taught me during the training sessions. On Friday night, in spite of my wavering faith, two persons received healings in their backs and both of them also received healings in their eyes. Three persons were slain in the Spirit."

The Rochester, New York Healing Explosion was different in flavor than any other one we've had to date. The most outstanding thing about the Explosion was the fingers that went out from it to various other regions. There was a group from Wooster, Massachusetts who had watched the video tapes and were now excitedly believing that God would bring us to that area next year.

There were people from Connecticut, Long Island,

Pennsylvania, Florida, Louisiana, Nigeria, Texas, Canada, Latvia, Belize, California and many other locations. Each person or healing team came with the vision of taking Healing Explosions back to their own city or country.

A Spirit-filled medical doctor is taking Spanish tapes and books to Belize for a medical missionary trip. We gave books and tapes to the Nigerian couple. The couple from Latvia are going to translate the book and video/audio into the Latvian language.

Friday, the day of the Healing Explosion, was also "Lend-A-Hand Day" in Rochester. We had a prayer meeting at the Seven Sister Cities Bridge and approximately 1,500 people attended. The mayor had written a welcome to us, but the councilman went to the wrong location so he didn't get to deliver it until the night meeting, but we had a wonderful time praising God. We prayed over the entire city as we called the people in from the north, the south, the east and the west.

The Holy Spirit spoke and told us to take up an offering for the Lend-A-Hand of Rochester, and their newspaper reported the following:

"Among the more unexpected events during Lend-A-Hand Day, Democrat and Chronicle reporter Barbara Isaacs and photographer Karen Mitchell were covering the 'Prayer in the Square' portion of the Rochester Healing Explosion slated for the War Memorial last night. Church officials set two empty guitar cases out for Lend-A-Hand donations, and Mitchell and Isaacs ended up carrying about $700 back to the newspaper offices in paper bags."

Rochester is over, but it will never be forgotten because of the rivulets that will reach around the world because of this one Healing Explosion.

Dallas, Texas was another excited turned-on city for Jesus when we arrived for the Dallas Healing Explosion.

The prayer meeting at noon at the Reunion Arena brought forth tremendous results as people shared their desire to take the healing message all over the world! As the tremendous crowd gathered, they unashamedly claimed the entire city of Dallas for the kingdom of God. As we faced the skyline of Dallas and repeated the Pledge of Allegiance, the American flag fluttered brilliantly in the sky. A Dallas businessman led a prayer for the city.

The Pledge of Allegiance was especially moving because of the international flavor of the Dallas Healing Explosion. Dr. Hong and Amy Sit from China, who now pastor in Houston, Texas, added an oriental touch. Knut Frohm and his wife from Sweden came with five other people, determined to take the Healing Explosions back to all the Scandanavian nations. Others came from the Comanche Indian tribe in Oklahoma, from Brazil, from Peru...

A young man from England said, "This is what my country needs!"

A woman from Mexico said, "Don't forget about your neighbors to the south!"

It was interesting to see the Swedes, the Chinese, the English, the Brazilians, the Indians, the Peruvians, the Mexicans, the Nigerians, and many other nationalities praying for each others' countries.

Then it was time for the Explosion! The spirit of praise and worship broke out immediately when the Greater Life Exalters brought the audience to such a high it seemed as if the roof would come off of the Reunion Arena. Everyone sensed something great was going to happen. The praise continued to crescendo and no one wanted to stop because they felt so close to Jesus.

Our four Dallas grandchildren had the best time of all! They think Healing Explosions are the greatest ever and all love to heal the sick!

We made a call for cancer patients and over 250 people came down for hands to be laid on them. It was a moment of power and faith as we personally laid hands on all of them. In all of the Healing Explosions, we have never seen such a burst of faith as was present during the healing of cancer. It was a special time for all present!

Then came the call for the baptism with the Holy Spirit! They poured out of the Arena seats to fill the floor and so many came that it looked as though almost all the seats were empty. People are hungry, hungry, hungry all over the world! And they received!

When the healing teams were released to heal the sick, the healings were tremendous! I personally laid hands on all those who had come because they wanted a baby and I was still going strong after I had laid hands on more than 300! There's going to be a baby boom in Dallas!

Finally, the last person who had come to have hands laid on them was ministered to! The Explosion was over, but the memories linger on and the waves that went out from Dallas will resound around the world!

We knew from the meetings months before the Indianapolis Healing Explosion that it was going to be a winner! From the first "live" training session at the Convention Center, faith was at an all-time high and so were the miracles!

For people who don't believe healings last, Gene Lilly surprised us with a visit. You may remember he was healed sixteen years ago in Orlando, Florida. He is a picture of health and happiness today. If you haven't read his story in the book *"DON'T LIMIT GOD"*, you should! He was dying when he came to one of our services! You'd never know it today, because the devil is a defeated foe and Gene is a perfect example of healings that last - and last - and last!

The special "Pastors' Anointing Service" on Thursday evening was attended by 261 pastors and their wives. They left anxious to return to their churches to turn them upside down!

When the actual night of the Healing Explosion arrived, the praise and worship seemed higher and sweeter than we have ever felt it before. The joy of the Lord filled all the hearts as hundreds came down onto the floor to praise God in the dance!

Then came the call for salvation and the baptism with the Holy Spirit! It seemed as though the entire arena literally emptied down onto the floor. The hunger is the same for the power of God regardless of whether we're overseas or in the United States! God is moving mightily!

The entire audience was so ready for healing that it seemed as if the Holy Spirit was directing us not to teach or anything - just release the healing teams. Within three minutes after releasing the teams to start ministering, there was a line nearly a block long of people wanting to testify to their healing. The teams were so ready, so prepared, so excited, it was one of the greatest nights we have ever seen. More people got out of wheelchairs than in any of the other central states Healing Explosions! This is but a little taste of what God is beginning to do in the end-times!

Chapter Fourteen

DON'T SMELL THE GARBAGE

by Frances

El Salvador and Guatemala are two nations physically close to the prosperous United States, but the poverty in many areas of those countries is heart-breaking!

As we were going to the meetings in Guatemala City, we went through the garbage dumps (we took a short cut) and saw people living right in the middle of the dumps. Each time a dump truck would come in, they would rush over to get the "fresh" garbage. The people were literally fighting over who would drag off the big sacks of garbage! They broke into them and clawed for anything and everything that looked like it might be edible.

Our hearts cried! I said, "Don't these people get sick from eating contaminated food?"

The driver said, "Yes, and they die right here in the dump!"

We were almost physically ill watching people who were ecstatic about anything they could put in their mouths regardless of how contaminated or rotten it might be!

God spoke and said, "This is the way so many of My people are! They are living in the garbage dump and eating the food of the world instead of sharing at the banquet table I have prepared for them!"

In a twinkling of an eye, God showed us that much of the world is living in a spiritual garbage dump, feeding themselves on the pleasures of the world instead of on the riches that He has planned for us.

As we drove through that garbage dump in Guatemala, I was reminded of a scripture I used many, many years ago when I was speaking to youth groups. "In a wealthy home there are dishes made of gold and silver as well as some made from wood and clay. The expensive dishes are used for guests, and the cheap ones are used in the kitchen or to put garbage in. If you stay away from sin you will be like one of these dishes made of purest gold - the very best in the house - so that Christ himself can use you for his highest purposes" (2 Tim. 2:20-21 TLB).

Because these young people got the garbage out of their lives, hundreds and possibly thousands of them chose to be a "gold plate" instead of a garbage can!

God has provided an everlasting and eternal feast for us in which we can partake right now! Too much of the Christian world has slept for two thousand years since Jesus gave the Great Commission and told us to all preach the gospel, cast out devils, minister the baptism with the Holy Spirit, and heal the sick.

As we taught in Guatemala, people who had never feasted at the great table of God watched miracles happen through their own hands. We saw people dropping the carnal things of the world and running after the blessings of God! Hundreds, even thousands, of people saw a world of milk and honey opening before their very eyes as they made their decisions to be obedient to Jesus and fulfill the Great Commission.

Since all Central American countries are not trouble free, the first thing that greeted our crusade team in San Salvador was machine guns and policemen. However, God's power was not stopped from moving in a tremendous way.

Upon our arrival Saturday night, we were driven to the home of some people who had taken the video healing training. A little boy listened to us talk for awhile and finally came to me and asked, "How come you have an accent now when you don't have it on the video?" He did not understand that the videos were all lip-synced into the Spanish language by Spanish people.

We started off on Sunday morning at a Catholic church. When mass was completed, the priest said, "I want you all to stay because Charles and Frances Hunter are going to have a Miracle Service." After we spoke about what God is doing today, we ministered the baptism with the Holy Spirit and ninety percent of the people there came forward "And they were all filled with the Holy Spirit and began to speak with other tongues, as the Spirit gave them utterance" (Acts 2:4). The healing teams worked with us and the healings were incredible.

That evening we visited an Assembly of God church and saw the same remarkable things happen. A woman came forward who had been scheduled for surgery on two ruptured discs in her back. However, she developed encephalitis and as a result they could not operate. She recovered from the results of encephalitis but her back problems remained. She was in excruciating pain and was carried to the stage moaning and groaning.

We laid hands on her, commanded two new discs to form in her back and her legs grew out. As we finished ministering to her, she jumped up and said, "I'm healed, I could feel the discs grow in and I don't have any pain at all." She then explained that she had also been suffering with severe neck pain - it had disappeared also!

The second person on the stage was a man who saw this tremendous healing. He also had severe back problems and a disease which was causing tremendous pressure and pain behind his eyes which would eventually lead to blindness. He was wearing bottle-thick glasses when he came up on the stage and when we sat him down to grow out his legs, that simple procedure that does so much to release God's power to cure back problems, he was instantly healed.

He stood up and said, "See what you can do for my eyes." We laid hands on his eyes, commanded that foul spirit of infirmity to come out in the name of Jesus, the blood and fluid to flow normally within the eye structures, and spoke healing and wholeness to both eyes.

When he fell under the power of God, his glasses flew off. As he stood up, he pointed at us and said, "You are not a doctor but I am. You cannot diagnose me, but I can." And he turned to the audience and said, "As a physician, I am telling you that I am completely healed!" Not only did he receive a remarkable back healing, but his eyes were perfect. He was being forced to retire from medical practice, but now was restored in body and soul!

The audience rose to their feet in a standing ovation. Unknown to us, he was a very famous neurosurgeon who had come "to merely inspect and to see what we did". When he saw the woman totally healed on the stage in front of his own eyes, it gave him faith to believe for his own healing.

He received the baptism with the Holy Spirit that night, attended our Healing Explosion training sessions the next day and was on a healing team at the San Salvador Healing Explosion.

The first person to whom the neurosurgeon ministered was a young man in a wheelchair who had been unable to walk. As a result of what the doctor had learned about healing, the young man was totally healed by the power of God and got up and walked.

One evening we had a Full Gospel Business Men's Fellowship meeting and while many people were healed, probably the most dramatic was a little girl who had cancerous lumps all over her body. I laid hands on her and the lumps instantly disappeared. The joy on the face of the mother was indescribable as the little girl said into the microphone, "Mother, it doesn't hurt anymore."

The crowds are the same wherever we go - hungry for the baptism with the Holy Spirit and the glorious expression on their faces showed that they were truly receiving what God had for them.

The San Salvador Healing Explosion saw hundreds of people healed and receiving the baptism with the Holy Spirit. It was incredible to watch these healing teams in action who had never seen a Healing Explosion, nor had ever met us but who learned the principles of healing through the Video Healing Schools.

Wherever we go the response is the same. People are turned on when they see the supernatural power of God and realize that they can do the same things themselves.

Our next stop was Guatemala, and when we landed, we went directly to a meeting of doctors in the hotel where we were staying. The response of the Guatemalan doctors was exciting. We asked a chiropractor to examine a man with back problems.

He said, "I can't do it without a table."

So we said, "Use the floor." He laid the man down on the floor and did his examination. It was exciting to see the doctors receive information about the supernatural healing power of God, and then to see him divinely healed in a second!

Our next stop was Antigua, the oldest city in Guatemala and the city called "the most Catholic in the world" (ninety-eight percent of the people are Catholic).

Interestingly, we were warned that if you minister with the Catholics in Central America, the Protestants won't work with you; and if you minister with the Protestants, the Catholics won't minister with you. But God's Holy Spirit can override all of these things, and did!

We attended a luncheon with some of the pastors of Antigua and the surrounding areas, and then had a small but very powerful Healing Explosion in Antigua. The children who received the baptism with the Holy Spirit cried tears of pure joy - they knew they had received the power of God in their lives.

From the beginning of the first training session, the miracles of healing came forth. The highlight was the healing of a person's leg which lengthened a full four inches. Polio had left its effects, but God's power made the person whole.

A woman came forward who had been born with two discs missing in her back. A doctor examined her and confirmed the diagnosis - the discs were missing. After we laid hands on the woman and commanded new discs to form, the same doctor re-examined her and was very excited to discover the discs were there - "laying on of hands" worked!

After one of the training sessions, we were privileged to meet the mother of the President of Guatemala. To reach her we had to pass through her tight security system - more sawed-off shotguns. We asked her through her interpreter, "Do you need God to heal you in any way?"

She said, "Yes, I have a separated shoulder which was the result of an accident." We ministered and she was totally healed!

Knowing she was a Christian, Charles began to talk about the baptism with the Holy Spirit because we didn't know whether or not she spoke in tongues. She said, "I'd love to receive the baptism with the Holy Spirit!" So I ministered. Immediately she was speaking fluently in her heavenly language.

Before we left this most gracious lady, we laid hands on her and she fell under the power of God. As we stood there, the same thought struck all of us, "What would happen if the guards came in with those sawed-off shotguns and saw her on the floor?"

Praise God they didn't come in! But what an exciting time and what an honor to be able to minister to such a great woman!

Then came the two Healing Explosions in Guatemala City, Guatemala. One on Saturday afternoon in one section of town and the second in another section across that sprawling city. Each was a duplicate of the other. As we sent the teams out to minister healing, people popped up from wheelchairs like popcorn! Some of the pictures of the event were difficult to believe. People had discarded their worn-out wheelchairs because they had been healed when the teams laid hands on them.

One of the most interesting things we saw in Guatemala was that the people believed us when we said the healing teams had the same power we did. We knew the message had gotten across when not a single person asked us to lay hands on them! They obediently went to the healing teams because they saw the results they were obtaining.

This is what God is saying in these end-times: It's the hour of the believer! So rise and shine!

Chapter Fifteen

NEVER A DULL MOMENT -
EIGHT NATIONS IN FIVE WEEKS

by Frances

January and February were months of supernatural anointing and strength from God. As we reflect on the trip, we thank Him for His constant supply of energy.

We went to Taiwan as our first visit to Asia for a Healing Explosion. The video tapes had been lip-synced into Mandarin and Cantonese (Chinese) languages and the book *"How to Heal the Sick"* had been translated and printed in Chinese. Several hundred Taiwanese had already completed the 14 1/2 hour video school and studied the book. They were excited about our arrival to guide them into their first great Healing Explosion!

We discovered the same excitement about learning to heal the sick as in every other nation. The training session was jammed to capacity, with over 1,350 people having been trained to minister in the great Healing Explosion, and their hunger and desire was unequaled anywhere. During the first session we ministered the baptism with the Holy Spirit and hundreds came forward with a zeal for everything God has.

The church was so jammed, we had people on four levels - the church level, the second level, the third and fourth floors. We had about thirty trained healing team members with us from the United States, so they spread out over the floors, and as we ministered on the first and second floors, they ministered on the other two. Growing out arms and legs works in Taiwan just as much as in any other place in the world.

They treated us to some interesting foods like squid, eel, and octopus, but we liked their spirit better! They are moving ahead full speed to get more of our books into the Mandarin language and are going at a rapid pace to get the tapes and books into mainland China where they have many openings.

The spirit in Taiwan is incredible because they are determined to preach the gospel around the world!

What a thrill to drive up to the Presidential palace in Taiwan at the exact moment requested - not one minute before, or one minute after - and be met by a greeter and an armed guard who snapped to attention when we stepped out of the car door.

Thanks to Nora Lam, we had an invitation to meet with Vice President Le Teng-hui, and have tea with him.

After walking down a red carpet which seemed to be ten miles long, we were ushered into the meeting place and given a diagram showing exactly where we were to sit.

At the exact moment, Vice President Le Teng-hui walked in, we all arose and then he invited us to sit down. We spent twenty delightful minutes talking about JESUS! He is a born-again believer, and we believe God is opening up mainland China for our ministry.

At the end of the time, he presented us with a gift, and then the official government photographer took our picture with him.

Down the long red carpet again, past the armed guards and into the limousine!

Five days later the former president died, and Taiwan now has a born-again Christian for a President. Hallelujah!

The Healing Explosion in Taipei, Taiwan was exciting! We had to have two meetings because of the response of the people! It was so thrilling to us to watch the Chinese lay hands on the sick, grow out arms and legs, do the "TTT" exactly the same way we do it in America, and have the same results!

Would you believe it is sometimes difficult for us to remember all the miracles that happen on a trip, because there are so many? Our Asian tour started with Taiwan, and from there we went to Japan.

Where only one percent of the population is Christian, the hunger in Japan is incredible! We personally hand-carried the first twenty sets of Japanese video healing tapes with us. They were not finished until one-thirty the morning before we left.

Over two hundred pastors and leaders had gathered together for our one-night stop in Japan, and to say they were excited is putting it mildly. Japan is going to see miracles like they never dreamed before as a result of this one meeting. (By the way, hamburgers were $12 each in Tokyo, coffee was $4.00 per cup, and a hotel room cost us $250.00 plus tax for the one night!) The couple that picked us up filled their car with six gallons of gas, and two quarts of oil, and the bill was $48.75.

When they introduced us to the pastors they turned on the video tapes, so the first words the pastors heard us speaking to them were in their native language. Praise God for modern technology!

Through an interpreter, I asked them if they would really like to know what the world says about the

Japanese. I then repeated the question to make sure they really wanted to know, and then I said, "The world says that the Japanese are the world's best marketing people, and once they get the message of Jesus, it will spread rapidly over the entire world, and then Jesus will be back!"

The people whom the world thinks are so stoic laughed so hard they almost fell off of their chairs!

After the one-night stop in Japan which told us they are going to run with the end-time message, we went to Hong Kong for one meeting.

We met three men from India on the big 747, and during the short trip from Japan to Hong Kong, they got healed, accepted Jesus, and received the baptism with the Holy Spirit! The man who was doing our video tapes for us was in the back of the plane ministering salvation and healing as well! Miracles follow wherever you go, if you'll just look for them!

In Hong Kong they said they had never seen arms and legs grow out, and it completely astounded them! Some of the Chinese men crawled on the floor to get between the crowd to see the miracles God was doing! The expressions on their faces was something to see!

A tremendous hunger was created in their hearts to learn how to heal the sick, and video schools are spreading all over that area.

From Hong Kong we flew to Manila. We had met a singing group from Sweden in Hong Kong and saw them again in the airport. We asked them to sing for us, and the anointing of God flowed through the airport as they sang and a lady sitting two seats down from me who was reading a book on the occult, screamed, "Shut up!" The Holy Spirit had so moved on her she couldn't stand it, and she finally got up and ran as fast as she could to get away from the presence of God!

When we landed in the Philippines, there was great excitement wherever we went. While we were there, God gave us some interesting words, one of which concerned the way the Philippines are going to take the gospel to every creature in their nation QUICKLY!

Over fifty Healing Explosions had been held since we introduced them a year before to the Philippines, and the masses have caught the vision of healing the sick.

One of the most interesting words God said to us in the Philippines was, "The talk of the streets will be JESUS! It will not be sin and the things of the world, but it will be Jesus!" This is for every nation in the world, but it depends on YOU! This is the hour when Christians are learning to talk about Jesus freely wherever they go.

What a mind-boggling thought, but what an exciting thing! We told the American healing teams who had gone with us to the Philippines to wear their healing team ribbons wherever they went, and the results were astonishing! The first two who left the hotel with their ribbons which proudly announced "Hunter Healing Team" discovered that they weren't two feet away when someone walked up to them and asked for healing, and before they had time to minister healing, a line formed with others hungry for the healing touch of Jesus!

The same thing happened to all the teams as they wore their ribbons in department stores and restaurants. They had lines forming wherever they went. Truly Jesus is becoming the talk of the streets.

The two Healing Explosions were really colorful because for the first time in the history of the Philippines, they had a typhoon in January. But the umbrellas went up and no one left, and it didn't dampen anyone's spirit. The first healing was a blind person!

The Filipinos are continuing with their Healing Explosions, and are seeing fabulous results! The stories and pictures we receive from those islands are thrilling because they show that these beautiful people have really caught the vision of the end-time ministry of the body of Christ!

We flew home from the Philippines for just a day-and-a-half before we left for South America. People have asked us how we keep from having "jet lag" and we tell them that we leave town before the jet lag has time to catch up with us!

Our first stop in Brazil was Belo Horizonte which started off super exciting with a 5 p.m. church service in a building under construction. It was packed out wall-to-wall and God was moving in a tremendous way. Suddenly a shower poured buckets of water all over us. However it did not stop the move of the Holy Spirit. Ninety percent of the people received the baptism with the Holy Spirit and as we walked through the audience, many people were also healed. We laid hands on two lepers. Even the healing of leprosy is possible with God!

Immediately following that service, we went to another church for a second surge of the Spirit of God.

It is impossible to list all of the miracles that happened at the Healing Explosion there, but here are a few to let you know God was moving!

A woman who hadn't walked for thirty-two years came walking up on the stage totally healed.

A man who had come in a wheelchair with spondylithiasis was healed as he walked up on the stage.

A little two-year-old girl who was a deaf mute is now talking and hearing as a result of a healing team member laying hands on her.

A deaf man was healed when a healing team ministered to him.

A demon-possessed woman ran through the audience violently hitting people. A believer stepped up and laid hands on her and the shocking look on the woman's face was amazing. (All of this was recorded on videotape.)

Billboards and signs were plastered everywhere in Brazil. The people said, "As we go by your picture every day, we lay hands on it and pray for you." We believe that a lot of the results we saw in South America was because of people who were praying for us.

The love there is absolutely incredible and the thing they said they loved the most about us was the love we have for people. Who could help but love people who have such a tremendous God-love on the inside of them!

This continent is coming alive because people have found that Jesus is alive and wants to live on the inside of them, walking and talking with and through them every day.

From Brazil we went to Cordoba, Argentina. The first morning we were there, the hotel manager welcomed us to his hotel and a few minutes later we led him into the baptism with the Holy Spirit. He said he was embarrassed to let us lay hands on him in the restaurant. We told him that we do this all the time. He knew one of his legs was an inch short, so we ministered to him and his leg grew out. He couldn't believe what happened. He was healed!

One pastor rode a bus for twenty hours to meet us in Cordoba. He went back home carrying video tapes and books to teach his people how to heal the sick. They had announced that we would be ministering to pastors, and their cry is the same wherever we go. They begged and begged, "Please give me a set of video tapes and books that I can take to start this in my town." A pastor was on the way to Chile because he knows the hunger that is there.

The Healing Explosion in Cordoba was another night of "impossible" miracles. There were about twenty thousand people jammed into a building with no air-conditioning, but God never seems to mind. Thousands were listening outside the building. We could hardly get up to the stage because of the press of people. Their hungry faces said they believed that God was going to heal them! It seems we hadn't said but just a few sentences when the power of God broke and people began passing wheelchairs over the top of the crowd. It was impossible to move, so when people were healed, you could tell by the screams from the crowd.

Probably the most exciting thing about Cordoba happened when the healing teams went to work after we left the building. The miracles were overwhelming. Our purpose in going to foreign countries is to teach them that they can do it, too. Many reports came back to us of miraculous healings that took place through the healing teams.

Then we went to Buenos Aires where we had some of the most exciting experiences of our lives!

Our second church service in Buenos Aires brought a big surprise. The building was so totally jammed with people that it took them almost fifteen minutes to get the two of us to the pulpit. It is hard for us in America to i-magine people so hungry for God that they will pack out an unair-conditioned church in one hundred degree weather and stand for four hours waiting for the service to start. Their hunger is so great there's nothing they want more than to just be where people are talking about Jesus and miracles are happening.

In a church which would normally hold two thousand people, nearly four thousand were jammed. The bodyguard assigned to me must have weighed about four hundred and fifty pounds. Without him I would never have gotten through the pressing masses and it was equally difficult for Charles.

The group of men who took us through the crowd actually looked like a football team on the offensive as they literally pushed the crowds to one side.

There were so many people left outside, we had to duplicate the meeting later in order to minister to everyone.

The power of God literally exploded in this particular church. The pulpit was on the second floor with an open area overlooking the first floor. The seats then went all the way from the second floor to the fifth floor in a very steep rise. The power of God broke and the Holy Spirit began to move in an unbelievable way! I looked down to the people on the lower floor who were in wheelchairs and I said in Spanish, "Silver and gold have I none, but such as I have give I unto thee. In the name of Jesus Christ of Nazareth, rise up and walk."

Over and over again, I said, "Receive your healing in the name of Jesus! Receive your healing in the name of Jesus!" The people began to come out of wheelchairs. We instructed the healing teams to go to every person in a wheelchair, minister to them and get them out. The people got up in almost a simultaneous arising! People who had not walked in years got up and began to walk.

One old man got up and was moving very slowly. He was obviously very crippled. A few minutes later, I noticed he was walking a little faster. The third time I saw him, he was running back and forth.

A little girl who had a spina bifida had never walked.

She also was healed and up walking around. Hallelujah!

Two reporters from *Avida Abundante* (a magazine which circulates through Argentina and Uruguay), interviewed us on our second day in Argentina. One of the reporters and their photographer had been at our meeting the previous evening. One of them mentioned that she had a problem with her spine.

We agreed to minister "TTT" (the total thing) and immediately began with "the neck thing". She explained she had a problem from the top of her spine to the bottom, especially in the hip area. When we started to do "the pelvic thing", one hip was three quarters of an inch higher than the other. As we commanded it to level up, the pain in her back totally disappeared. By the time we finished ministering "the arm thing" and "the leg thing", she was feeling great.

Then I said, "I want you to practice on your friend."

We had been explaining to them the principle of multiplying the healing message by training others to minister healing - we teach somebody else, who teaches somebody else, who teaches somebody else. We instructed her to lay hands on the second girl's legs which were about one inch difference in length. Immediately the short leg shot out.

Amazed, she replied, "I did not believe it when it happened to me, but when I did it to my friend, then I believed."

Then we had the second young lady stand up and discovered her pelvis was lower on one side. As the other reporter laid hands on her, the hips evened up and she was totally healed. The first reporter said, "I believe, I believe, I believe!"

We told the second reporter that it was now her turn to lay hands on their photographer because we weren't going to depend upon one person knowing how to minister, one "star" to do all the healing.

We asked him if he had anything wrong with him and were shocked to discover he had been in an accident in 1984 which had severed the tendons in his left leg. Because gangrene had done some severe damage, he still suffered great pain while walking. Even to touch it caused electric shocks through him.

What an opportunity and a challenge for our new "baby" healing team member who had never laid hands on a single person! Charles gave the commands in English, they were translated into Spanish by one reporter and then said a second time in Spanish by the reporter who was ministering to the man's leg. As the commands were made, the leg grew out.

We spoke a creative miracle for the tendons to be healed and then Charles asked the man if he would like to take the elastic stocking off his leg. He was absolutely overcome with joy as he discovered there was no pain in his leg. He said nobody could even touch his leg and Charles had run his hand all the way down this man's leg and there was NO PAIN! He spent the next few minutes jumping up and down on his leg because he could not believe the miracle that had happened to him.

This is multiplication! Every believer needs to teach somebody else how to heal the sick!

We asked him if he had any additional illness in his body. He replied, "No, but my mother does." So we all laid hands on him and through the prayer of agreement, we spoke healing into her. We laid hands on his hands and anointed him to go and lay hands on his mother for her healing.

That night as we were riding down a bumpy street in a hot, unair-conditioned mini-size taxi cab, we came upon a big theatre loudly proclaiming the movie "FATAL ATTRACTION"! The theatre was obviously not open, because there was a line stretching two or three blocks in each direction with people standing five and six across.

Our hearts literally cried out as we said, "God, let there become such a hunger in the hearts of people that they will line up like that to hear about Jesus!" All I could think of was the churches in America which have so many empty seats at every service.

The taxi driver turned and said, "That's where you're speaking tonight! They're waiting to hear you talk about Jesus!"

We almost fell out of the car and raced across the street to discover the theatre was filled to capacity with standing room only! We had to have *three piggy-back services* to minister to the entire crowd in a theatre with no air-conditioning and no windows.

Praise the Lord, the "Fatal Attraction" was *Jesus* as people died to self and were born again by the Spirit of God!

We were not prepared at all for what happened on the day of the Healing Explosion! Before we left for the meeting, we received a call telling us that the stadium was already filled and the doors had been locked. People were lined up for blocks trying to get into the service. Many had traveled twenty hours only to be turned away at the gate.

When we walked into the stadium, our hearts cried as we realized how God can use two people who have never been to a seminary or had any formal training and yet are just available to the things of God. The officials estimated there were over fifty thousand in the stands. Every seat was filled!

As we walked onto the field, the crowd rose to their feet shouting "Jesus! Jesus! Jesus!"

If you've never heard that name said by fifty thousand people in unison, you have missed an exciting thrill. It does something for you that you can't describe.

At least forty thousand received the baptism with the Holy Spirit. When this many people are in total agreement and in one accord as they began to speak in tongues, there is an explosion of power. People were healed all over the audience.

The way the stands were built prohibited many people from coming down onto the field. There were some twenty thousand on the field at the end of the meeting, but the police finally made them stop because of the press of the crowd. We instructed the healing teams to minister wherever they were.

We would hear a shout, "Somebody over here is out of a wheelchair!"

Then there would be another shout from the other side of the stadium, "Somebody over here is getting out of a wheelchair!"

As we stood under a beautiful moon, we saw the power of God surge through the believers of Argentina.

There are some times and some events you can never put into words, nor is there any way you can ever express what you saw and felt. It is too overwhelming to attempt.

To see crippled bodies healed all over an audience at the same time because of some simple teaching the people have received is more than we can understand, but how we praise God for what He is doing around the world today as He prepares us for the return of Jesus!

People are so hungry they met us wherever we went and they had the knack of finding us wherever we were, too! After the Buenos Aires Healing Explosion, an old

truck loaded with probably thirty people on the open bed
came by the hotel to ask us to personally lay hands on
them!

Wherever we go, we are able to minister to people in
motels, airports and hotel rooms. One transfer between
planes required a forty-five minute car ride. Instead of
taking a cab, a local businessman volunteered to drive us
in his comfortable car. We discovered his entire family
was there and he requested that we minister to all of
them. Right in the middle of the street and/or sitting on
the curb, we did "the pelvic thing", "the neck thing", etc.
until his whole family was healed.

We discovered during our trip that he didn't have the
baptism with the Holy Spirit so Charles ministered the
baptism right in the middle of the busy Buenos Aires airport.

From Buenos Aires we went to Porto Alegre, Brazil,
which was the site of another exciting Healing Explosion. Because of an airline strike, it took twelve hours
(instead of a short hop) to reach Porto Alegre (translated
means "Happy Port"). We were met by approximately
thirty local pastors and wives who presented us with
flowers and thanked us profusely for coming. They told
us immediately that they expected God to do great things
in their city.

The man at the front desk of the hotel wrote us a note
telling us he had tinnitus in his ear. He was sure if we laid
hands on him that he would be healed.

I laid hands on him first and commanded the spirit
of tinnitus to come out and the blood to flow normally.
The sound was still there. Charles then did "the neck
thing" - and he was totally and completely healed. He
was crying as we ran out the door to go to the Healing Explosion with tears of thanksgiving for what God had

done.

The manager of the stadium said, "In the history of the stadium, there have never been that many people inside." The estimated crowd was twenty-two thousand with many more on the outside watching via a video screen. He also commented that he had never seen such a beautiful orderly crowd in his entire life.

There were very few there who had previously received the baptism with the Holy Spirit so when we gave the call, the response was overwhelming.

The floor was already covered with people so they had to stand at their seats for the baptism with the Holy Spirit. At least ninety percent of the audience was standing to receive the power of God in their life.

After Charles ministered, they all began to speak in one accord producing a very loud power-packed sound. The many pastors who participated all said the same thing - they had never seen anything like this in their lives.

After the baptism with the Holy Spirit, the power of God was so strong that people would not stop praying in other tongues. They continued as we instructed the people in the wheelchairs "to get up and walk in the name of Jesus". Healing teams began to minister to the people and many people came out of their wheelchairs and started to walk.

Before long, a deaf mute had been healed and was now saying, "Mama", "Papa", "Baby" and was hearing perfectly.

Crutches were passed up onto the stage. Many braces came forward over the heads of the people.

A young girl was squealing with excitement as she walked for the first time in her life. Many children who had never walked were healed and walking around the

stadium that night. A young boy was running all over the
place while everybody around him rejoiced.

Not one person moved or left the auditorium until
after we had left. They weren't going to miss out on a
thing!

The pastors were jumping up and down with excitement as they watched God move through their country-
men. They cried out to us, "Please, can we have videos?
Please, can we have videos?" Our hearts were touched!

We're saying, "God, speak to the people who read
this. Speak to the people who support this ministry.
Reach their hearts as poignantly as You have reached
ours."

Our hearts are crying out to supply all of South
America with all they want and need.

With a sound of a mighty rushing wind still in my
heart and in my spirit, we were sitting in our hotel room
after the fabulous Healing Explosion in Porto Alegre,
one of the most European cities in South America. It was
reported that the people there would not be as responsive
as they are in other places because they are more
Americanized and Europeanized. In all of our Healing
Explosions, I do not recall ever feeling the power of God
as intense as we felt it that night, nor the people more responsive.

Sometimes in a land of plenty such as in America, we
forget the whole world does not have the gospel as we
have it. These people are crying for books, they are crying for video tapes, they are crying for cassette players so
they can use these tools and learn about a living miracle-
working Jesus and how He can work through every believer. They are hungry!

At the breakfast table in Porto Alegre, the day of our
Healing Explosion there, the man who had coordinated

activities for us in Argentina and Uruguay, shared an exciting story that happened during one of the video training schools.

An ambassador in Uruguay had had the first joint of his little finger cut off when he was small. After watching the teaching on creative miracles at the video school, the teams ministered to him and commanded the finger to grow back. Nothing happened that night, but fifteen days later, a perfect little finger had grown back. Many people are discouraged and let doubt and unbelief come in to destroy their faith when a miracle doesn't happen immediately. Don't let that happen to you!

A very interesting story involved a Lutheran pastor's son who was running the video in a school in Porto Alegre. His father smoked and so did he. One of the men in the church said, "How come he's smoking? God doesn't like that."

The other person said, "Well, many pastors in that denomination do smoke so we're not going to say anything."

Then they watched the hour of video teaching where we show the miracle service. A young man was chewing gum and I took the cigarettes out of his pocket and the gum out of his mouth so he could receive the baptism with the Holy Spirit. When this Lutheran pastor's son saw this he began to cry. He came up and gave his cigarettes to the pastor saying, "I'll never smoke again." We never know what little thing we say or what little thing we do will influence a whole denomination.

On to Montivideo... There are no large churches in Uruguay. As we understand, Christianity basically got its start approximately three years ago, so the churches are very small and hold no more than two or three hundred at the most. Knowing this we did not anticipate or expect as large a reception as we received in Buenos Aires. The population of Uruguay is three million, 1.3 million of which is in Montevideo.

The local workers had rented a stadium that would normally hold about ten thousand people in the stands. When we arrived, we were told there was not an inch of space left in the entire auditorium to stand. They had to lock the doors one hour before we had arrived - again shutting many people outside.

The head of the Assembly of God and the head of the Church of God of Uruguay both said the same thing, "Never in the history of Uruguay has there been a Christian meeting as large as this one." They estimated approximately twenty thousand were there. Who knows how many there would have been had they not had to lock the doors.

While we were there, a carnival was also going on nearby. Even though they drew tremendous crowds, it was nothing compared with the Christian excitement in Uruguay because of the Healing Explosion. All the cooperating pastors said, "Uruguay will never be the same. I can't believe what happened during these meetings!"

The healing teams were positioned in front of the stage near all the people in wheelchairs. First we gave the command, "Silver and gold have we none, but such as we have, we give unto you. In the name of Jesus Christ of Nazareth, rise up and walk." Then we turned to the healing teams and said, "Get them out of the wheelchairs!"

There was an explosion of power we will remember as long as we live. An eight-year-old girl in a wheelchair had never walked in her life. After being ministered to, she was not walking perfectly, however she was up and walking and knew she was healed. They brought her up on the stage and someone reached out to help her. She shoved everybody away because she wanted to show everyone that she could walk by herself.

People held up crutches all over the great stadium because there was no way they could make their way through the crowd. You could see the crutches waving in the air and you could see the people walking out of the wheelchairs in a great demonstration of the unbelievable power of God.

South America has a revival going on which we do not believe will stop until Jesus Christ comes back again.

Now for our final explosion on this trip.

Brasilia is the capital of Brazil. Until twenty-five years ago, Rio De Janeiro was the capital. However it was extremely inefficient for the operation of government facilities so the government bought millions of square meters of land. The park itself contains four million square meters and was opened in 1978.

They bought all of this land in the middle of a plains area. There was absolutely nothing there. They called in an architect who designed the city in the shape of an airplane and it's one of the most unique places you've ever seen.

None of the streets cross each other. Wherever two streets meet, one goes under and one goes over. They have allowed acres and acres of land for parkways in between buildings and freeways.

Some of the officials of the government provided a bus for us to visit the Senate and the House of Representatives which is a very unusual building.

This is the most modern city in all of Brazil and the most unique. The nose of the plane is the seat of the government buildings. In the cockpit of the plane which forms Brasilia's pilot plan, is located the Ministries Mall, having at the back, the Plaza of Three Branches. There are located the seat of the Executive, the Legislative and the Judiciary branches of the Federal Government. There are ten tall rectangular shaped structures lined up side by side in the Mall. Each is for a different branch of the Government. It is without a doubt the most efficiently planned capital in the entire world.

It's the only place in Brazil where we had the feeling of not being cramped and pressed in and squeezed in on all sides because they allowed sufficient room for everything.

It's very unique because they have what they call the North Side and the South Side. All the hotels in the city are built in one area either on the North Side or on the South Side. It's a duplication across the road. All of the sports facilities are in one location. There is no other.

All the judicial buildings are together in one area. There is no other. The shopping centers are all in one area and there is no other area to shop.

Brasilia has been plagued by a spirit of religion, they told us, ever since it opened and there has been actually very little move of the Spirit there. However, we had over two thousand trained workers and the Healing Explosion brought some incredible results.

It was covered by the local television station who recorded many of the miracles and talked to many of the people as soon as the miracles happened.

Of all the cities we were in it was probably the most difficult to get started because many of the churches here don't even allow you to clap in church. However, after about twenty minutes, it was amazing what happened to the audience and when we released the healing teams, the entire auditorium went absolutely wild. People got up out of wheelchairs and wheelchairs passed up to the stage over their heads. A girl who went back over to the auditorium the morning after the Healing Explosion told us,

"I wept because I could not believe the crutches and the braces and the walking sticks and the wheelchairs that were left at the auditorium." A silent witness of the power of God through believers!

Chapter Sixteen

WE HAVE A "WAY"
WITH REPORTERS

by Frances

Here are two stories we are utterly compelled to share with you, because they happened to two newspaper reporters who came to our services total skeptics, but for some reason or other, changed their minds!

Candy Nail was a cynical, hard as "nails" reporter from a Miami newspaper. How she got involved with us is an interesting story, and we'll let her tell you exactly how it happened!

"I had just changed jobs, but after a few months, I again became dissatisfied. The political arena was exciting, but it just wasn't what I felt called to do. One night I was working late in the office, staring at thousands of xerox labels. I was bored, bored, bored. I said, 'God, if you don't do something, I'm going to make such a mess of my life that I'll never be able to fix it!' I felt like an idiot, talking to the air. At age 31, I was pretty sure that the devil existed, but not God. I left the office, went by a bar and had a drink, and went home.

"Three days later, I had to go make a copy of a business meeting report. Our copy machine was broken, so I took it to a print shop: their equipment was broken, so I took it to another shop. They were busy, so I had to take it to *another* place! There was a lady there who was picking up a stack of fliers: she handed me a paper that was advertising an evangelistic meeting with Charles and Frances Hunter.

"I took the flier back to my office and threw it on my desk. My boss came out, saw it, and said, 'You're not going to that, are you? Those charismatics are in the occult!' I didn't know what charismatics were, but I was all for the occult. I decided to attend the meeting, but for the purpose of writing an article for our newspaper, exposing 'faith healers.' The paper had a small, but politically powerful, circulation.

"At 7:30 p.m. on June 1st, I roared up to the meeting, flipped the butt of a joint out of the car window, and swaggered inside. I was in a bad mood, and sat all the way in the back, by the door. I was used to church services where somebody tinkled a piano and we all sang every verse of 'Just As I Am,' so when the drums and guitars cut loose and people started dancing in the aisles, singing 'He is Jehovah,' I knew this was not a normal group!

"I sat poised, pen in hand, waiting for the Elmer Gantry stuff. Frances Hunter got up to preach, and I had never seen anybody like her! She made claims about Jesus that I *knew* couldn't be true. Then she asked whoever didn't have the baptism with the Holy Spirit to raise their hand. Well, I certainly didn't want anybody to think I was one of these crazies, so I put my hand up. I instantly took it down as ten people said, 'I'll go up there with you!' 'Oh, no you won't' I snarled. 'Get away from me!'

"I saw one tall, blond teenage boy walk in with crutches: his left leg was visibly curved, and shorter than his other leg. All of a sudden, I saw a big commotion up on the stage. The blond kid was running back and forth, holding his crutches over his head, and I saw that his leg was perfectly straight! Aha, I thought, A RUBBER LEG!!! I also saw Charles Hunter pray for a lady who had been having upper back pain. They had her extend her arms out in front of her, palms together. They began to pray, and I saw one of her arms become about five inches longer than the other one. (I was watching her shoulders, and they didn't move!) Frances ran over and said, 'Charles, you've ruined her!' Everybody laughed, and her arms became equal again. I was absolutely horrified! People laughed for a week about the look on my face.

"I was back the next night, still sitting in the back by the door. I liked the music. I liked Charles and Frances Hunter. What I didn't like was the God they were talking about! I was uneasy, but still knew that my Satan was stronger than their crucified Jew.

"I came back for the final service. I got real brave, and moved up several rows. There was more music, more testimonies, and more preaching. I sat there and held a mental conversation with myself: 'Well, it looks like they're for real. No, they can't be. Well, what about the people that got healed? They're just planted in the audience. I don't believe in healing. I won't believe it until it happens to me, and it won't happen to me because I'm not getting *near* those people!' I wrote it all off as mass hysteria and mental suggestion. *I* didn't see anything, *I* didn't feel anything, and *I* only trusted *me*.

"Frances gave an altar call, and nearly everybody in the place stampeded forward. I sat alone in the audience. I looked around in back of me, and was startled to see a cloud filling the back of the auditorium. I thought the place was on fire, and started to get up and leave. Charles Hunter pointed at the cloud, and said, 'Look! The glory cloud of God is in this building!' I heard someone say, 'Where? I don't see anything!' As I watched the cloud roll forward, my mouth fell about forty-five inches, and I sat back down.

"When the service concluded, I went out to the lobby to write the article for the paper. I was deep in thought when I looked up to see the minister who had sponsored the meeting, David Southwell. He began to ask me what I was going to write, what I thought about the Hunters, and what I thought about Jesus. I tried to get rid of him, but he just wouldn't leave.

"All of a sudden, I began to feel real funny - and looked up to see Charles Hunter walking up. Now, I'm not a timid or easily frightened person - but as he got closer, I began to actually shake. Here I was in a hotel lobby, with people looking at me, and when Charles laid his hand on my shoulder, I sort of bent over and yelled, 'No! Don't touch me!' I was amazed that I was acting this way. Charles and Frances kind of backed up and stared at me, and gave Reverend Southwell a look that said, 'You handle this one.' They were late for a meeting and left.

"David asked me, 'Do you always shake like that?' 'No.' 'Do you like feeling that way?' 'No.' 'Do you want to fix it?' I looked at him and said, 'You don't understand. I'm not from your religious background.' And I told him just what religious background I was from. I expected him to either run for the exit or get up in disgust, but he didn't. He said, 'I'm going to pray for you, and God is going to fix this.' I know he prayed the sinner's prayer, but I don't remember much else he said.

"A sharp pain went through my back when I stood

up. David asked what the problem was, and I told him. 'Sit down,' he said, 'God can fix that too.' I was skeptical, but sat back down. David held both legs by the ankles, and noticed that one leg was nearly an inch shorter than the other one: I already knew that from the orthopedic surgeon. He began to pray: 'In Jesus' name, I command this back to be healed. I command this leg to grow out to the correct length, and for the muscles and bones and tissues to be strengthened. In Jesus' name, I command all pain to be gone and your body to be perfectly healed. Thank you, Jesus!' For the second time that night, my mouth fell as I actually felt *my* leg growing! I stood up and bent over - there was no pain!

"I went out and sat in the car and tore up my notes. To top off the evening, as I drove home I ran out of gas and had to walk."

...But her life was changed!

Sometimes what looks like the world's darkest situation can turn into one of the brightest!

Jamestown, New York looked like the most dismal meeting we'd ever had in our entire life. Before we left the hotel, the TV reporters were encouraging everyone to stay home, because the temperature was sub-zero, and the snows made travel difficult. The evangelist always has to go, whether or not anyone else is there, so we donned our snow boots and plowed through a six-foot mound of snow to get to our rental car which was almost hidden because the snow plows had really piled up some big stacks of dirty "white stuff."

We drove down the slippery street to the old movie theatre where our meeting was to be held, climbed over the snow mounds again, and got inside of the theatre. At least, we should say, through the first doors of the old theatre. We had to wait for quite a while before they opened up the doors, and there was no heat in the foyer where we were standing, so our bodies were below normal temperature when we finally entered the building.

It was no better inside! I tried to find someone who worked for the theatre to tell them that the heat wasn't on, and when I finally located someone, they told us the sad news that the furnace had broken and there would be no heat that afternoon.

Still wearing our coats and boots, we tried to set up our book table, but the theatre had been painted completely black, and in the entrance where our books were to be sold, there was one little fifteen-watt bulb hanging down from an electric cord. We couldn't even see the colors on our books it was so dark and we've often wondered what books the people got! It would be a miracle if they got what they asked for, because we could not read any of the titles.

Still shivering, with our teeth chattering, we went inside to look at the theatre. What a shock! What a damp, dismal auditorium this was! We've spoken in a lot of peculiar places, but this was the worst! The only light on the black-painted stage was again a little fifteen-watt bulb which hung from the ceiling!

The people in the city were certainly television oriented, because they listened to the newscasters and stayed home in droves. Finally, somewhere between seventy-five and one hundred people showed up and sat there shivering.

It's really hard to get into praise and worship when your teeth are coming together in a staccato beat because of the cold, but we tried a few songs anyway! During the weak praise and worship, I whispered to Charles, "What are we doing here?" I was sure I had missed God because

I knew He would never send us to a place like this!

One thing God has taught us over the years is to give every service "everything we've got" regardless of the size of the crowd or the circumstances, and that's just what we did, even though we did dismiss the service a little quicker than normal just because we didn't want a bunch of frozen corpses out in the audience. They were all sitting there with their coats pulled up tightly around their necks, but people who have problems don't need that kind of care, so we started laying hands on the sick quickly.

After we had laid hands on everyone there, we packed our books rapidly to take back with us. We were the last ones to leave the theatre and as we waded through the black snow still piled waist high in front of the theatre, we looked at each other, laughed and said, "Can anything good ever come out of Jamestown?"

About a year later I received a copy of a newspaper from Erie, Pennsylvania, which had one of the funniest stories I'd ever read, and it was written by someone who was asking the same question we did, "What are we doing here?" Let me tell you their story, just to prove that God can take any mess and make a miracle out of it.

Jack Grazier was a newspaper reporter for the Erie, Pennsylvania DAILY TIMES. He and his wife Debbie had been trying to have a baby for several years, but with no success. They had tried all the medical techniques, and the article said that his wife even bought him oversized boxer shorts, because that was supposed to be helpful in cases like theirs.

Some friends "drug" them to the meeting, and he wasn't impressed with anything he saw or heard. His description of me was so hysterical I won't even tell you what he said, but he described Charles as a "withered, staid looking, aging Republican!'" That didn't turn me on, but nevertheless, I continued reading the article!

This couple had never been to a charismatic service, and of course were not prepared for what was about to happen. As people came forward and climbed up some of the most broken-down stairs I've ever seen, we began laying hands on them and they began falling under the power! To someone who has never seen this, it can be a tremendous shock! I remember what I thought when I went to a Kathryn Kuhlman service and saw this for the first time. It almost blew me away because it was beyond my ability to understand how she could "do" it!

This couple was sitting out there with the same thoughts. They decided they were not going to go up onto that run-down, gloomy, depressing stage just to fall down and get their clothes dirty! Their friends kept encouraging them since they had driven so far to at least "try" it and see what happened. They decided to come up onto the stage, but they vowed that they would not fall down!

The first one I came to was Debbie and when I asked her what she wanted, she began to cry and said she wanted a baby! I immediately said, "That's my specialty. I have them in all colors - red, black, white and yellow." Her husband immediately panicked because he wanted to make sure they got the right color! The reason I said that is because God has given me a very precious anointing in this area and wherever we go, there's always a baby boom shortly after that!

I laid hands on her and said, "Father, your Word says that the womb of your children will never be barren, and that you cause the barren woman to be the joyful mother of many children. I ask you to place in this womb a beautiful baby, perfect, whole and delivered within one year, in the name of Jesus!" Then I said, as I always do, "And if it's twins, you have to name them Charles and Frances!" Then I added, "Remember every good and perfect gift comes from God!"

Debbie did just what I expected her to do and what she never expected to do! She fell out under the power of God! Can you imagine the shock of her husband when he saw her lying on the floor? I turned to him and said, "What do you want Jesus to do for you?" He later told me he mentioned the fact that he had some sort of arthritis of the chest, so I laid hands on him and commanded the spirit of arthritis to come out in the name of Jesus! He fell under the power without a catcher behind him! He said the next thing he remembered was looking up at a black ceiling with a tiny little bulb hanging down.

They told us later that they "wobbled" off the stage in a dazed condition because they had never experienced anything like that in their entire lives!

They went home, completely baffled by the entire afternoon. How could they have fallen down when Jack had braced himself against being "pushed" over? Nevertheless, it had happened, so they decided to practice at home. He got in front of the sofa, took the same stance he had taken at the theatre, and said, "Go ahead, push me!" Debbie pushed with all her might, and he still didn't fall down. They tried several times, but she could never make him fall down. They began to wonder, was there really something to this supernatural power of God?

God's Word never returns void, because on April 22, 1986 a beautiful little boy named Ian Christian was born. Jack shared the fact that when he tells the story of how they got pregnant, people look at him and ask him if he really believes that God had anything to do with it, and he says, "I know the mind can do strange things. Coincidences can happen. But, though it was hard at first for me to admit it, yes, I do believe that Frances Hunter and a divine power channeled through her did it!"

The thing that thrilled me so much was when I read the article, it shared about how he was standing in the birthing room holding the baby in front of a picture which had the inscription, "God's Gift!"

If the story ended right there, it would be a fabulous story, and it would have made the trip to Jamestown worthwhile, but it didn't stop there! McCall's Magazine picked up the story and printed it in the October, 1987 issue. From that, *Good Morning, New York,* the television show starring Regis Philbin which is watched by twelve million viewers asked us to be guests, and we had a wonderful time sharing Jesus on the program with Jack and Debbie. Before the program, however, they both received the baptism with the Holy Spirit!

As a result of all this, Jack has been commissioned by one of the world's largest publishers to write a book on legitimate faith healers!

The article in McCall's appeared in the occult section, and many Christians were upset, but if you could read the mail we have received, it would thrill your heart because it came from people who would have never read the article if it had appeared in a "religious" column.

Signs and wonders will always follow you if you'll just be obedient to God and go wherever He tells you to go. This is a miracle that will never end because even as we are drawing close to finishing this book, more miracles are in the offing because we didn't turn and run away from a miserable, damp, dark, old, delapidated theatre building! God always has something good in store and always has signs, wonders and miracles "up His sleeve!"

Chapter Seventeen

CATCH THE VISION

by Charles

Little did we realize that from video taping a little Bible School would come the tool God is using to train hundreds of thousands, soon hundreds of millions, of ordinary believers to do signs, wonders, and miracles.

We just read again the vision God gave to Frances in 1980 which is recorded in the first chapter of our book, *"How to Heal the Sick"*. God had clearly spoken to our hearts concerning this end-time message of miracle evangelization of the whole world. Now this vision is being fulfilled and implemented in every continent, every nation of the entire world.

God showed Frances rivulets of silver and gold running into all sorts of odd little places. As He began to reveal its meaning, we wrote "The more we examined this divine vision, the more we began to understand that God was telling us to take the total message of salvation and healing to the entire world by letting the masses learn how to operate in the supernatural and to heal the sick.

"Then the picture expanded even more, and we saw the video schools going into ALL the world - into the small places were evangelists never go, to teach all the people in the remotest places of the world how to lay hands on the sick and heal them. The students who learned from these video tapes would then go out and preach the gospel to the poor, heal the brokenhearted, preach deliverance to the captives and recovering of sight to the blind, and set at liberty those who are bruised."

As God developed this end-generation training, He began to have us prepare it for use all over the world. To reach the world with video or audio tapes and books, they must be converted into the languages of the world.

The first Healing Explosion was held in Pittsburgh, Pennyslvania on July 4, 1985, and this began a move of God throughout all the earth. There have been at the time of this writing scores of Healing Explosions which we have conducted. But in the Philippines alone, there have been more than that conducted by people we have trained, and by people they have trained, and by people those have trained. Making disciples with video training seems strange but the proof of it being God's chosen tool is that it is working, and it is being taken all over the world supernaturally and supernaturally fast.

In the late fall of 1985 God said to put it into the Spanish language and He opened the great healing training in Colombia, South America. Then in Minneapolis one Saturday afternoon in a motel room, Frances was talking with leaders in the Philippines; I went to another phone and was talking with some people from Zaire, Africa, about the French language. As soon as we completed those calls, both excited about what we saw God expanding in fulfillment of the vision He had given us, Frances said, "God, why did you choose two such old people as we are to do this giant work?" God's reply was simply, "Because you are 'dumb' enough to do what I tell you to do!" What God was saying is that we were always willing to be obedient regardless of what our natural minds might be thinking!

Since then the books have been translated and

printed (or in the process of being completed) and the video tapes translated and either lip-synced or overdubbed into languages so over 80% of the poplulation of the world can take the training in their native languages. That's over four billion of the earth's population of five billion souls! That's a remarkable miracle and only God could have accomplished that in such a short time. Now God is implementing the distribution and training with these tools and they are now in every continent of the world and almost every nation of the world. God is opening ministries into which the tools are being implanted.

As we sit and look at a world map, our spirits leap with excitement and joy at the rapid and extensive move of God in such a short time. Take a look at the world map, look at each continent, then focus on individual nations; then focus on cities, towns, and villages; then look at the individuals who are being touched by Jesus, and being endued with God's Holy Spirit power and made into common, everyday, miracle-working disciples in each spot on planet earth and be astounded, overwhelmed and amazed with us.

Then take a moment to consider how very close we are to the return of Jesus. We cannot help but feel a closeness to Jesus in working with Him to reach all the world and every creature on earth with this great news.

Jesus came to earth to save the lost and left us with certain promises which He *spoke into existence* and they must come to pass before His very soon return.

Paraphrased, His message for the final harvest of souls in preparation for His return for the Church: He told us that the gospel would be preached to every creature on earth (five billion) by ordinary believers doing signs and wonders so people would believe and be saved, and when this is accomplished, HE WILL RETURN!

Hallelujah!

We see the Day of Pentecost as a prototype or model of the end - time Church, just as it was in the beginning of the Church. What happened to them, we believe, must happen to the entire Church before the return of Jesus. They received the baptism with the Holy Spirit to give them power and make living like Jesus and doing His works like He did possible.

"Then there appeared to them divided tongues, as of fire, and one sat upon each of them" (Acts 2:3). We believe this was the purging, purifying fire of the Holy Spirit which burned the old selfish, fleshly, carnal nature into nothing but dead ashes, making a place for Jesus to take total control of their lives to live in and through them in His holiness and purity.

Peter, who loved Jesus so much, had just denied and cursed Him because Peter thought more of his own life than he did that of Jesus. But when the fire came down on him, Peter's old self-nature died and he could truly say, like Paul, that "I have been crucified with Christ; it is no longer I who live, but Christ lives in me..." (Galatians 2:20).

Jesus declared that we were to "Pursue peace with all men, and holiness, without which no one will see the Lord" (Hebrews 12:14).

"Husbands, love your wives, just as Christ also loved the church and gave Himself for it...that He might present it to Himself a glorious church, not having spot or wrinkle or any such thing, but that it should be holy and without blemish" (Ephesians 5:25 & 27).

Two things must happen before the return of Jesus:

1. The church must be a holy church (the baptism with fire).

2. The gospel must be preached to every creature on

earth by ordinary believers doing signs and wonders so they will have an opportunity to believe in Jesus.

What we have very briefly summarized in this book is just a drop of what is actually happening all over the world as His great army of believers are learning that they can operate daily wherever they live, work, play, or exist in the supernatural power of God just as the early Church disciples did in the New Testament.

We pray that as you read this book of Chronicles of this hour you will feel the enormous move of God that is taking place before our eyes, and will accelerate until Jesus' return. We MUST catch this vision and become an active part so much that we put this as the first order of importance in our lives. It is not something that can wait.

THE TIME IS NOW!

Chapter Eighteen

THE HEART CRY OF GOD AND JESUS

by Charles

Throughout this book we have written of great healings and other supernatural miracles. We have mentioned over and over again the tremendous move of God through the hundreds of thousands of people coming to the Healing Explosions and crusades being saved and receiving the baptism with the Holy Spirit.

We have described many people getting out of wheelchairs because that perhaps is the most impressive miracle in a Healing Explosion, in a church service, or in a shopping mall. Literally hundreds of thousands, perhaps millions of miracles other than wheelchairs being emptied occur through the hands of those disciples of today who have learned how to dispense God's wonderful miracle-working power to heal the sick in the name of Jesus.

Jesus said, "...But you shall receive power when the Holy Spirit has come upon you; and YOU SHALL BE WITNESSES...to the end of the earth" (Acts 1:8).

People who loved God and Christ Jesus during the past 2,000 years must have wanted to do miracles for Jesus. They just did not know how. When you pray repeatedly for healing miracles and they only happen once in awhile, there is not a confidence to step forth and say this miracle will happen. But this has been because of the

simple lack of knowledge of how to release God's Holy
Spirit power to do the healings. Through this simple
training tool God has made this understanding com-
monplace, and hundreds of thousands are, or soon will
be, doing miracles daily wherever they go.

The great healing schools and Healing Explosions
are simply training grounds and launching pads to get all
believers confident that they can preach the gospel, cast
out devils, minister the baptism with the Holy Spirit,
handle the powers of darkness, and lay hands on the sick
and heal them for the glory of God in Christ Jesus to be
Jesus' witnesses!

As you have lived through these mighty moves of
God chronicled in this book of Acts of today, see yourself
doing the same things others are doing who have learned
how to release this mighty power of God. Jesus meant it
when He told all of His believers to be just like Him and
do the same things He did and even greater things.

How Jesus must have looked forward during the
past 2,000 years to seeing this move of God come into
being all over the world! How very excited He must be
right now to see this long awaited age come into being!
And we are only seeing the tip of the iceberg, the very beginning of what He is about to perform through His host
of miracle-working believers who have caught His vision
and committed their lives to do what He wants done -
QUICKLY!

As you have read these wonderful miracles around
the world done through the hands of ordinary believers
like Peter, James, John, Paul, Mary, Bill, Susie and
Frank we pray that you will see Jesus alive as never before. We pray that you will see His very purpose for giving His life so people all over the world will believe in
Him and be saved.

We pray that you will catch the vision of His end-time wrap-up plans to reach all five billion souls on earth today by His blessed willing believers taking His place to do His works by His miracles.

We pray that every person who meets Him and gives his or her life totally to Him to be His bond servant will become in reality His body, to be like Him in character, in loyalty to Him, in willingness to forget themselves and let Him live in and through them in utter abandonment of desire for earthly things or earthly pleasures.

We pray that each believer in Jesus will see clearly and realize clearly that Jesus is coming very soon and that we are to be His holy Church and to be the powerful, excited, "determined-to-win" army, doing even greater things than He did while He was on earth in a human body like ours. He is very alive and very real and very personal to each of us, so much so that when He is Lord of all, nothing else matters on this earth except to let Him live freely in each of us.

Time is short and we have a lot of work yet to do before His return. When He said to us, "What you do, you must do quickly", we heard His voice and are pouring every ounce of energy and every second of time into accomplishing all He wants done. He already knows the exact moment He will return, and He will be on time, and everything He plans to accomplish He will, and He will do it primarily through His believers.

We pray that every pastor will catch the vision Jesus had and realize and do their responsibility to equip and mature their people for this great, thrilling work of which we are privileged to be a part, to be the center of, to have the responsibility for.

We pray that the focus, the purpose for existing, the total reason for being a church or a Christian, will be to

reach every creature, every person anywhere we can
with the gospel of Jesus. All programs of every church
must support the purpose of our existence - to win people
to Jesus and to make them into miracle-working disciples.

To be a Sunday school teacher and not a soul-winner
and not a disciple is purposeless. To be on the board of
Elders, Deacons or Trustees has no meaning unless every
function is a united purpose to do the works of Jesus in
order that some may know Him. Every youth worker,
every children's worker, every adult worker must have
as their center purpose to make their people, young or
old, into alive witnessing disciples who will produce
fruit for Jesus. All other purposes are fruitless, yet necessary, unless their purpose and focus is on preparing
people to do the works of Jesus quickly.

The very heart cry of God and Jesus must be what is
happening on earth through believers today. The very
heart cry of each of us believers should be to move with
uttermost sincerity and haste to perform all Jesus assigned to us. The world is so very lost, and we believe
they have been prepared by the Holy Spirit to search for
Jesus, but they don't know where to find Him. With great
dispatch we must produce hosts of miracle-working disciples to reach them quickly. What the early disciples
did, we must hasten and enlarge and move with greater
power than even they did.

God said, "For the earth will be filled with the
knowledge of the glory of the Lord, as the waters cover
the sea" (Habakkuk 2:14).

That is what is happening right now. This knowledge of the glory of God is rising up in people to glorify
God by doing what Jesus commanded.

When we see what He has accomplished in just these

short years which are the beginning of the end before the return of Jesus, we stand in awe of His greatness and swiftness. When in about three weeks we saw possibly a quarter of a million people receive the baptism with the Holy Spirit and speak in other tongues as the Spirit gave the utterance, we know the earth is being covered with His glory quickly. When we see tens or possibly hundreds of thousands of ordinary believers catching the vision of Jesus to harvest the world for His return, we know He is coming soon. When we see great multitudes being healed and not just one evangelist doing the ministering of healing, but Jesus' body doing it like He foretold, we know the earth is being covered with the glory of God.

Catch this vision!

A lot of people were caught up in the great move of God on Azusa Street at the beginning of this century. Most people missed it.

This miracle evangelization by ordinary believers being witnesses with power wherever they go daily is the other end of Azusa Street. Some will get caught up in the move of God. Some will not.

Those who do will be like the man who built his house on a rock and it stood through the storms. Those who miss being doers of His Word will be like the man who built his house on sand and it fell when the storm came.

We have a choice! You have this choice!

It won't be long before the return of Jesus and we must become that great army of witnesses to gather in this great harvest of souls before Jesus arrives!

What more can we say than "LET'S GET THE JOB DONE FOR JESUS NOW!"